POLITICAL REALITIES
Edited on behalf of the Politics Association by
Bernard Crick and Derek Heater

ELECTIONS
Second edition

POLITICAL REALITIES
Edited on behalf of the Politics Association by
Bernard Crick and Derek Heater

Elections

Second edition

Iain McLean

Longman

LONGMAN GROUP LIMITED
London
*Associated companies, branches and representatives
throughout the world*

©Longman Group Ltd 1976
*All rights reserved. No part of this publication
may be reproduced, stored in a retrieval system
or transmitted in any form or by any means, electronic,
mechanical, photocopying, recording or otherwise,
without the prior permission of the copyright owner.*

First published 1976
Second edition 1980
ISBN 0582 35323 8

*Set in 10/12 Times by
Woolaston Parker Ltd*

*Printed in Great Britain by
Spottiswoode, Ballantyne Ltd, Colchester*

Titles in the Series
Political Studies: A Handbook for Teachers
Contemporary Political Ideas
Modern Bureaucracy: The Home Civil Service
Law, Justice and Politics
The Commonwealth
Issues in British Politics Since 1945
Parliament and the Public
Elections *Second edition*
Parties and Pressure Groups
Local Government
Government and Politics of Northern Ireland
The Cabinet and Policy Formation

Contents

Acknowledgements

We are grateful to the following for permission to reproduce copyright material:
Macmillan, London and Basingstoke, and St Martin's Press Inc. for two tables from *Political Changes in Britain* 2nd edn, by D. E. Butler and D. Stokes. Reprinted by permission.

Political Realities: the nature of the series

A great need is felt for short books which can supplement or even replace textbooks and which can deal in an objective but realistic way with problems that arouse political controversy. The series aims to break from a purely descriptive and institutional approach to one that will show how and why there are different interpretations both of how things work and how they ought to work. Too often in the past "British Constitution" has been taught quite apart from any knowledge of the actual political conflicts which institutions strive to contain. So the Politics Association sponsors this new series because it believes that a specifically civic education is an essential part of any liberal or general education, but that respect for political rules and an active citizenship can only be encouraged by helping pupils, students and young voters to discover what the main objects are of political controversy, the varying views about the nature of the constitution – themselves often highly political – and what the most widely canvassed alternative policies are in their society. From such a realistic appreciation of differences and conflicts reasoning can then follow about the common processes of containing or resolving them peacefully.

The specific topics chosen are based on an analysis of the main elements in existing A level syllabuses, and the manner in which they are treated is based on the conviction of the editors that almost every examination board is moving, slowly but surely, away from a concentration on constitutional rules and towards a more difficult but important concept of a realistic political education or the enhancement of political literacy.

This approach has, of course, been common enough in the universites for many years. Quite apart from its civic importance, the teaching of politics in schools has tended to lag behind university practice and expectations. So the editors have aimed to draw on the most up-to-date academic knowledge, with some of the books being written by university teachers, some by secondary or further education teachers, but each aware of the skills and knowledge of the other.

The Politics Association and the editors are conscious of the great importance of other levels of education, and are actively pursuing studies and projects of curriculum development in several directions, particularly towards CSE needs; but it was decided to begin with A level and new developments in sixth form courses precisely because of the great overlap here between teaching in secondary school and further education colleges, whether specifically for examinations or not; indeed most of the books will be equally useful for general studies.

Bernard Crick
Derek Heater

Preface

This is a book about elections. It deals with the way we choose MPs in Britain and possible changes in the method we use; with the ways people vote and their reasons for doing so; with the relevance of elections to democracy. It is *not* a book about the issues discussed in elections, and it deals only in passing with the political controversies that sometimes give rise to elections and are always argued about at election times. These topics are covered in *Issues in British Politics since 1945* by Leslie Macfarlane, in the same series as this book. It is hoped that the two books will complement each other.

I should like to thank the University of Newcastle upon Tyne for allowing me a period of leave of absence in order to complete this book, and my colleagues in the Politics Department for sharing out the burden of my work while I was away. I am also grateful to Nuffield College, Oxford, for its library and its hospitality.

My thanks go to Hugh Berrington and Jonathan Brown, who read earlier versions of this book and whose comments were very valuable. I should also like to thank Professor Berrington for permission to use Appendix 1, which is derived from an example of his (and ultimately, although much altered, from Rowland Hill, the versatile Victorian who not only invented the postage stamp but also pioneered progressive education and electoral reform).

For the second edition, I have revised the book to take account of some important recent developments, especially the Westminster and European elections of 1979 and the referenda on devolution in Scotland and Wales which took place earlier in the same year. I should like to thank all my students, both in Newcastle and in Oxford, who have helped me to think more deeply about the subject-matter of this book. The responsibility for what appears here is, of course, mine alone.

1 Elections: how and why

A British general election observed

At 12.48 p.m. on 7 February 1974, the Jimmy Young Show on Radio 2 was interrupted by the announcement that a general election would be held on Thursday, 28 February. Earlier that day, the Prime Minister, Edward Heath, had gone to Buckingham Palace to ask the Queen to dissolve Parliament and issue a writ for new elections. Her Majesty having "graciously consented", a Proclamation dissolving Parliament and providing for the election of its successor was published. A writ was issued to the returning officer for each constituency, asking him "to cause election to be made according to law of a member to serve in Parliament for the said constituency".

The legal machinery creaked into action. Parliamentary hopefuls who had found ten people in the constituency willing to sign their nomination forms, and £150 deposit to be forfeited if they did not receive one-eighth of the votes cast, had to be nominated by 18 February. If validly nominated, their names appeared on the ballot paper, with a description of themselves in not more than six words. This description usually took the form of naming their party, something which has only been permitted since an Act passed in 1969 belatedly recognised that political parties exist. Before this, voters had to work hard to remember which candidate belonged to which party, and never harder than in Anglesey in 1964, when they had to choose between Mr J. E. Jones, the Conservative candidate, Mr E. G. Jones, the Liberal, and Dr R. T. Jones, the representative of Plaid Cymru.

On 28 February 1974 a vast army of local government employees, schoolteachers and others descended on polling places all over the country shortly before 7 a.m. to lay out the necessary requirements: a sealed ballot box, a copy of the Electoral Register, several books of

ballot papers, two or three wooden screens (to allow voters to cast
their votes in privacy) and some pencils. In the following fifteen
hours, 78·1 per cent of the registered electorate cast their votes. At
10 p.m. the polls closed; in urban areas the counting started straight
away, while in country areas the ballot boxes were brought from
outlying towns and villages to a central point ready for counting
to start the next morning. The traditional race to be the first constituency to declare its results was won by Guildford. One of the ways
in which television has transformed British elections is in the
momentary importance it gives to mayors and local government
officials up and down the country, as millions of viewers wait for the
announcement of local results. Enjoying his fame to the full, the
mayor of Guildford intoned the formula, "I, being the Deputy
Acting Returning Officer for the aforesaid constituency, do hereby
declare that the total of votes cast for each candidate was as follows".
The list which followed showed a Conservative lead savagely cut by
a big increase in the Liberal vote, but was not in itself any real guide
to the final outcome. In the end, 301 Labour members were returned
and 296 Conservatives – neither party thus having an overall
majority of the 635 seats in the House of Commons. The balance
was held by 14 Liberals, 9 Welsh and Scottish Nationalists, and 14
others (mostly Ulster "Loyalists"). Mr Heath started negotiations
with Mr Thorpe, the Liberal leader, to see if they could come to any
agreement on a coalition or pact. When the talks came to nothing,
Mr Heath resigned and Harold Wilson emerged for his third term of
office as Labour Prime Minister.

This brief account of a recent general election has omitted almost
everything of interest. It is the aim of this book to try to fill in the
gaps. A general election is not only, or even mainly, a legal or
constitutional occasion. It is an event of unique political and
sociological significance. It is brought about (largely but not entirely)
by the decisions of a few score politicians, and its result is determined
by the decisions of 25 or 30 million voters. The reasons for their
decisions are often complex and deeply rooted, and their significance
is immense. We might, therefore, usefully look again at the narrative
of the February 1974 election, in order to put it into its proper
political context.

In the beginning the issue was simple. The Conservative government had a statutory wages policy restraining annual wage increases

to £1 plus 4 per cent a year. The National Union of Mineworkers rejected a pay offer of the maximum it was allowed under this formula and started an overtime ban which drastically cut the supplies of coal to power stations. The Government declared that, in order to economise in using the reduced energy supplies, industry must be put on a three-day working week, with some firms having electrical supplies from Monday to Wednesday, and others from Thursday to Saturday. (One point that was never settled was whether such drastic restrictions were really necessary in view of the level of coal stocks at the time.) The deadlock was not broken; instead, the miners voted on 4 February to turn their overtime ban into a strike. As one Conservative MP then said: "The miners have had their ballot, perhaps we ought to have ours." In these circumstances the election was called.

From the Conservatives' point of view, the issue was clear: it was the Government against the miners – the country against the miners, they might have preferred to say. Should a powerful group of workers be allowed to destroy the incomes policy of the government of the day? In reality, things were not so simple: every well-informed person knew that whichever party was elected would then have to settle with the miners outside Phase Three of the government's wages policy. This was pointed out with icy clarity by the Conservatives' most spectacular defector, Enoch Powell. Describing the election as "fraudulent", he added that it had been called "to secure the electorate's approval for a position which the Government itself knows to be untenable, in order to make it easier to abandon that position subsequently". But the Conservative leaders were bolstered by private opinion polls commissioned by the Conservative Central Office which showed that public opinion supported the idea of an incomes policy.

However, like many governments before them, the Conservatives in February 1974 discovered that they could start an election off on an issue which favoured them, but they could not keep it concentrated on that issue. During the course of the campaign the miners' strike receded more and more into the background, and other issues, especially inflation, came to the fore. The public did not have nearly so high an opinion of the Conservatives on the inflation issue as on the miners – they tended to think that Labour was more likely to keep rising prices down. The Conservatives' strong position was eroded as inflation and rising prices became more and more prominent at the expense of the miners.

During all this period, two entirely separate election campaigns were being fought. In London, politicians held their daily round of press conferences and radio and TV broadcasts. With their eyes closely fixed on the opinion polls they reacted to the issues that emerged and tried to create new ones favourable to themselves. But in the country an entirely different election was being fought. In parts of the United Kingdom, the Labour and Conservative parties were relatively less important. The Scottish National Party and Plaid Cymru (its Welsh equivalent) were putting up strong challenges in their respective countries. And in Northern Ireland politics was organised along quite different lines. There were splits between Protestants and Catholics, and between "Loyalists" who were not prepared to be loyal to the British government and others who were. The dominant political group in Northern Ireland, the Unionist Party, had previously been allied to the British Conservative Party, but their ways had parted – a fact which makes it harder now than it used to be for the Conservatives to gain an overall majority of seats in the United Kingdom, especially since the number of Ulster seats in the House of Commons was raised in 1979 to eighteen. Few people noticed at the time that if the Ulster Unionists had still been part of the Conservative Party, it would have "won" the February 1974 election, as it would have had 306 seats to Labour's 301. But *during* the campaign, the issues which aroused most passion in Ulster, Wales and Scotland were barely even mentioned by the politicians at Westminster. Furthermore, the election was one big battle made up of 635 little battles in the individual constituencies. In many ways, the battle in the constituencies was quite unrelated to the battle at the centre, and it owed more to very ancient traditions of election-eering going back to the eighteenth century and beyond than to anything connected with radio, TV, or the modern party system.

In the days before mass parties as we know them now existed, MPs were often local notables. Even if they were not local land-owners or squires they could still get to know and be known by most of the voters in the small electorates that existed before the nineteenth-century Reform Acts. Thus campaigning was largely a matter of public meetings and of canvassing for support among the voters. These traditions persist in the much altered conditions of today.

The public meeting as a form of electioneering is undoubtedly on the decline, as the national campaign on radio and TV becomes more important – perhaps for many politicians the "phone-in" programmes which have recently become popular are the nearest thing we now have to a public meeting. Many candidates in towns and cities hold few traditional public meetings or none at all, although they all try to meet as many voters as they can at factory gates or in shopping precincts. In country areas, the public meeting often still thrives, especially in towns and villages which still preserve a genuine communal life against the onslaught of television. In places as far apart as Montgomeryshire and Caithness meetings addressed by candidates in scattered villages can still attract 100 or 200 voters, and electors' personal knowledge of candidates and their personalities seems to be much greater than in the cities.

Canvassing is a traditional activity on which candidates of all parties place even more stress. At one time the point was for the candidate to meet every voter. This has been impossible for many decades now. The average constituency contains about 60,000 voters, which means about 30,000 households. If we supposed that a candidate canvassed for twenty days, and spent six hours of each day actually talking to voters on their doorsteps (thus allowing no time for him to get from one doorstep to the next), at a rate of two minutes per household, he could meet 3,600 households, or 12 per cent of the total electorate. In fact, of course, candidates usually meet far fewer voters than this. Most canvassing is carried out by party organisations on candidates' behalf. All parties stress that their purpose is not to convert doubtful voters, but to locate their supporters. Again, this must necessarily be so. No party has so many voluntary workers at election time that it could send canvassers to argue with every doubtful or hostile voter, and it is not clear that it would be worth the effort even if anybody could do so. What every efficient election agent hopes to have at the end of a canvassing campaign is a marked-up copy of the electoral register, on which all the voters are marked as for, against, or doubtful. On polling day, he should arrange to call on all the "fors", to find out if they have voted[1] and to cajole them to the polls if they have not. This is

[1] An efficient agent can do this by having number-takers, or "tellers", at the polling stations. Their job is to record the polling number of everybody who votes (if the voters are willing to give their numbers to the tellers). These numbers are then crossed off on the numbered list of "Fors", and those who have not voted are then "knocked-up".

known as "knocking-up", and is a characteristic feature of British elections which has few exact parallels in other democracies.

In February 1974, as at every other general election, all the major parties were busy with these time-honoured activities of speeches, walkabouts, canvassing, and knocking-up. How much difference did it all make to the election result? It is tempting to say: very little. Observers often comment that swings are pretty uniform in well-organised and badly-organised seats, in safe seats and marginal. Seats where party officials, when approached before the election, say that their organisation is particularly good or particularly bad never seem, on the day, to deviate very far from the general trend. The Common Market referendum of June 1975 reinforces this point. Both main parties were split into pro-Market and anti-Market factions; therefore neither was involved in any of the traditional activities of canvassing and knocking-up. Nor were these activities carried out by the pressure groups that sprang up on both sides. And yet the turnout at the referendum, at 64 per cent, was not much less than at a general election. Does this not show that canvassing and knocking-up are a waste of time, continued only because people love tradition, or because election workers would be lost without something to do?

This is not quite a knockdown argument. The election of February 1974 was one in which there was everything to play for in the campaign itself. The main parties entered the campaign neck-and-neck in the opinion polls, and there was a very large body of voters who were not committed to either. A party which could get them out might just tip the balance. Local studies show that, while canvassing and knocking-up are no use at *converting* people, they can be useful in dragging reluctant voters to the poll. If a voter is hesitating between casting his vote on a wet February night and staying at home to watch TV, the arrival of a party canvasser with the offer of a car to take him to the polling station may just be enough to persuade him to come out and vote. Furthermore, one area where there is no doubt at all that organisation matters is the postal vote. Voters are entitled to vote by post in either of two circumstances: if they have moved to a different constituency since the electoral register was drawn up; or if they are unlikely to be able to cast their vote in person on polling day. This last covers several categories: the old, the sick, those whose jobs mean that they may be away on polling day (long-distance lorry-drivers, for instance), and those living in a few extremely remote places where access to the polling station is physically difficult. There is a rather puritanical rule that postal votes are *not* allowed to people who are on holiday on polling day.

Generally speaking, the Conservatives are much better than anybody else at securing postal votes for their supporters. It is a complicated task which requires an organisation continuously on the job and not just at election times, and this the Conservatives are more likely to have than any other party. They are richer, and they have far more full-time agents than anybody else. Besides, as with any other sort of complicated official form-filling, middle-class voters – the sort most likely to vote Conservative – find the business of applying for a postal vote easier than do less articulate working-class voters. Many scores of thousands of people, especially the old and the sick, who would be entitled to postal votes, do not have them. At every election, and February 1974 was no exception, a small number of results depend purely on the postal vote. About ten seats, where the winning Conservative's majority was much less than the number of postal votes cast, were probably won by the Conservatives purely on their superiority at mobilising the postal vote. This may seem trivial. But ten fewer Conservative seats would have meant ten more Labour ones; the parties would have been separated by twenty-five seats instead of five, the result would have appeared much more decisive for Labour, and the next election might have been several years later, instead of only eight months.

Short-term and long-term factors

Canvassing, knocking-up, and public meetings are examples of activities designed to influence the election result during the campaign itself. As we have said, in February 1974 the three weeks' campaign, with its steady shift in emphasis away from the miners and towards inflation and rising prices, was probably decisive in bringing about the result it did. There were sufficient last-minute changes, such as Conservative voters switching to the Liberals, or people who had intended to abstain actually coming out to vote Labour, to guarantee that the result on 28 February was quite different from what it would have been a week earlier or a week later. But very many of the forces determining how people vote are unrelated to the short-term pressures of the campaign. As a voter, I may have made up my mind how to vote yesterday, or a year ago, or perhaps thirty years ago when I first got the vote; and the events which made me decide the way I did may go so far back into the past that nobody now living has any personal recollection of them. It is by no means a fantasy to claim that voting patterns in, say, Cardiganshire are connected with Welsh politics at the time of Lloyd George sixty years ago, or even that voting behaviour in Caithness and Sutherland is still affected by the traumatic Highland clearances of 150 years ago.[1] In later chapters we shall try to explore some of the deepseated forces which play such a vital role in determining the result of every general election.

The actual result in February 1974, as we have said, was very close. But it had other remarkable features besides its closeness. The Liberals' share of the vote leapt from two million to six million, their highest total since 1929. In seat after seat, especially in the south of England, they swept Labour into third place. However, in the British electoral system, this did them no good at all. Since each seat is simply awarded to the candidate with the largest individual total of votes irrespective of the performance of the other candidates, there are no prizes for coming second. The Liberals' six million votes and countless second places did them no good at all in the short run: they got only fourteen seats. The only comfort they could draw was that the result seemed to show how unfair the electoral system was, and therefore to add force to the demands which the Liberals have been making for many years to change to a fairer system, in which seats are won in proportion to votes cast.

In this introductory chapter, we have looked at some of the interesting questions raised by what went on at one particular election. What makes people vote in the way they do? Does the campaign make any difference? What is the role of opinion polls in an election? What is the effect of the voting system in use in Britain today? The rest of this book will be devoted to trying to answer some of these questions.

[1] In 1970 the writer asked the agent of one of the parties in Caithness what were the main issues in the constituency. Without hesitation, he replied, "the Sutherland clearances". These took place between 1817 and 1822. But they brought about a hatred of absentee landlords, and by association the Conservative Party, which still affects voting behaviour in Sutherland.

2 The Electoral System

The present system

For many years, the electoral system in Britain has come under strong attack – usually from its victims. The system, often referred to as "first-past the post", simply provides that the candidate with the largest number of votes wins the seat. All other considerations are ignored, such as how many candidates there were, how many electors abstained from voting, and whether the successful candidate got over 50 per cent of the votes cast. This system is straightforward and easy to understand and operate. It deals out a sort of rough justice when only two parties are in the running. But when three or four are struggling on more or less equal terms, it can lead to results that seem to be unfair, or at the very least somewhat anomalous. In the general election of 1970, for example, the Labour candidate for Cardiganshire won the constituency with 33·4 per cent of the votes cast, the rest being fairly evenly split between Conservative, Liberal and Welsh Nationalist candidates. An even more striking result was East Dunbartonshire at the general election of October 1974, where the Scottish Nationalist (SNP) candidate won the seat with 31·2 per cent of the votes cast – less than one-third of the total. Most cases are not as extreme as these two examples, but there is no doubt that the first-past-the-post system does introduce some curious quirks and distortions in the process of picking out the 635 successful candidates for the House of Commons. In the general elections of 1974 more MPs than ever were elected with less than half of the total votes cast; in October 1974, no less than fifty-six out of the seventy-one MPs for Scotland were elected on a minority vote.

However, the most important effect of the system is slightly paradoxical. Up to a certain point it is very hard for a new party to win any seats, but beyond that point it is very hard to stop it. This is often described as the "threshold" effect, and it is best illustrated by giving an imaginary example. Suppose I set up the Truth, Justice and Freedom Party to fight the Labour and Conservative Parties, and I persuade a quarter of the voters all over the country to support me. I may still end up with no seats at all. This may easily be seen if we consider three seats, all the same size with 40,000 votes cast in each, one of them safe Labour, one marginal, and one safe Conservative:

Party	Safe Labour	Marginal	Safe Conservative
Labour	20,000	15,000	10,000
Conservative	10,000	15,000	20,000
TJ & FP	10,000	10,000	10,000

With a quarter of the votes, the new party gets nowhere. But now suppose that I redouble my efforts until at the next election the Truth, Justice and Freedom Party gets just over a third of the votes. Then the tables are dramatically turned:

Party	Safe Labour	Marginal	Safe Conservative
Labour	17,000	12,500	8,000
Conservative	8,000	12,500	17,000
TJ & FP	15,000	15,000	15,000

My new party has comfortably captured the marginal seat and is hot on the heels of the major parties in seats where they previously outdistanced their nearest rivals by two to one. The threshold which a new party must cross in order to establish itself is therefore generally put at about 33 per cent of the votes, although, as we shall see later, this formula is too simple to apply straightforwardly to the real world.

The British electoral system is also sensitive to very slight movements of opinion between leading parties, because the swing of a relatively small proportion of votes from one party to another can result in a large number of seats changing hands. This is connected with a phenomenon called the "cube law". A study of a series of election results showed that when votes were cast for the major parties in the proportion A:B, they won seats in the proportion $A^3:B^3$. In other words, a given majority in terms of votes would be much exaggerated in terms of seats. If a party won twice as many votes as its rival, for example, it would take eight times as many seats, since if $A:B=2:1$, then $A^3:B^3=8:1$. In many of the famous landslide elections of the past there was surprisingly little difference between the leading parties. In the Liberal triumph of 1906, which ushered in Britain's last Liberal government, the Liberals took 400 seats and the Conservatives only 157; but the Liberals only got 49 per cent of the votes cast and the Tories 43·6 per cent. Even if one counts the Labour votes in with the Liberal total (since the two parties had a pact not to oppose each other in this election) the main parties were much closer together in terms of votes than of seats. Again, in 1945 Labour swept in with 393 seats to the Conservatives' 213; but Labour's share of the votes cast was only 8 per cent more than that of the Conservatives. Indeed, in British elections the two leading parties have almost always been very close (though there is nothing in the cube law to say that they must be). In the United States it is not uncommon for Republicans and Democrats to be 20 or 30 per cent apart in a presidential election; in Britain, nothing remotely like this has happened this century except in the National Government landslide of 1931.

The general election of 1979 resulted in a wide margin (by British standards) between the parties, with the Conservatives getting 74 more seats than Labour; but their shares of the vote were only 7·2 per cent apart, as the Conservatives got 45 per cent of the votes cast and Labour got 37·8.

Thus the arithmetic of the electoral system itself produces a number of distortions. When this is combined with the effect of the distribution of different sorts of voters around the country, the distortions may become still greater. For instance, "safe" Labour seats are usually much safer than "safe" Conservative seats. This is because the sorts of people most likely to vote Labour (such as Welsh miners) are more concentrated into small localities than the sorts of people most likely to vote Conservative (such as stock-brokers). This is nothing to do with the arithmetic of election systems, but simply a fact about the distribution of the British population. But it causes Labour to pile up enormous majorities in its safest seats, with the result that it usually takes more votes to elect a given number of Labour MPs than to elect the same number of Conservative MPs. This was the main reason for the anomalous result of the general election of 1951, when Labour got more votes but fewer seats than the Conservatives. (This historic injustice was redressed in February 1974 when the reverse happened. The bias against Labour we have just described did operate, but it was overlaid with new factors in the other direction so that in the end Labour got *fewer* votes but *more* seats than the Conservatives.)

The distribution or concentration of voters also has a crucial effect on the operation of the threshold principle mentioned earlier. The Truth, Justice and Freedom Party could gain no seats at all with its 25 per cent of the national vote, because its supporters were evenly spread across the country. If they had been concentrated in one or two places, the party would have done much better. The effect of this is clearly shown by the fortunes of the various minor parties in the general elections of 1974. In February, for instance, the relationship between votes and seats was:

Party	Votes	Seats	Votes per seat
Liberal	6,063,470	14	433,105
SNP	632,032	7	90,290
Plaid Cymru	171,364	2	85,682
United Ulster Unionist	366,663	11	33,333

The Liberals got six million votes but only fourteen seats because they were too thinly spread across the country. There are one or two areas of traditional Liberal strength – for instance parts of rural Scotland, Wales, and south-western England – and many of their fourteen seats were in these areas. But elsewhere the Liberals were piling up respectable votes in seat after seat (often up to 30 per cent of the votes cast) but never enough to oust the major parties.

The Liberals have only the doubtful consolation that their failure to gain a fair proportion of seats when their position improves may be matched by tenacious survival when their position deteriorates, as it did in 1979; their total of votes declined to four million, but their 14 seats only dropped to 11 because *sitting* Liberal MPs mostly did disproportionately well.

But whereas the Liberals were dispersed, the Scottish and Welsh Nationalists and the Ulster Loyalists were concentrated. Each was fighting seats only in its particular corner of the United Kingdom. (A proposal by some Scottish Nationalists to stake a claim to Berwick-on-Tweed, wrested from Scotland by Edward I in 1296, was not pursued.) Thus each of these three parties could score substantial gains. Indeed, after the second (October) election of 1974, there were actually more nationalists in Parliament than Liberals – fourteen as against thirteen. In October 1974, the Scottish Nationalists very nearly crossed the elusive threshold. They took over 30 per cent of the Scottish vote to the Conservatives' 24 per cent. They won eleven seats and came second in 42 others. Only four or five per cent more of the Scottish vote would have brought them spectacular rewards, but in the end the system defeated them. When their vote slumped in 1979, their seats plummeted to two. The system had helped them to rise further than the Liberals; now it kicked them down more brutally, and they were not even saved (as the Liberals were) by loyalty to sitting tenants.

The Welsh Nationalists, on the other hand, benefited from the concentration of their supporters *within* Wales. Plaid Cymru appeals most to Welsh-speaking, chapel-going citizens in north and west Wales, who favour keeping the pubs closed on Sundays. Many Welshmen, in urban south Wales particularly, are somewhat wary of these objectives, and in Wales as a whole Plaid Cymru did not do very well in 1974 – less well than in 1970, in fact. But the heart of Welsh-speaking rural Wales consists of only five parliamentary constituencies, three of which have been held by Plaid Cymru. Welsh-speaking Welshmen and Ulster Protestant Loyalists are two small groups who, because of their geographical concentration, have gained, not lost, from the British electoral system.

Possible alternatives
Nevertheless, those who do badly out of the system are bound to draw more attention to themselves than those who do well. But none of their main demands have been granted; after all, parliamentary majorities consist, almost by definition, of those who do very nicely out of the present system. Moreover, many people genuinely feel that any other system would produce weak minority governments or force

unstable coalitions upon Parliament. However, the British government has now introduced a proportional system for several elections
in Northern Ireland. And the elections held in June 1979 for the
British members of the European Assembly produced an embarrass-
ingly unproportional result. The Conservatives then got 50·6 per cent
of the vote and 77 per cent of the seats; Labour received 33 per cent of
the vote and 22 per cent of the seats; the Liberals, with 13·1 per cent of
the vote in Great Britain, got no seats at all, but the Scottish
Nationalists, with 1·9 per cent of the vote, got one. Not even the
traditional justification of first-past-the-post – "it produces strong
governments" – was relevant, since the British section of the
European Assembly is not the government of anywhere. Therefore
proportional representation is now an inescapable issue. Five main
alternative systems have been proposed. They are: the second ballot
system, alternative vote (AV), the party list system, the additional
member system (AMS), and single transferable vote (STV).

Under a second ballot system the election is split into two parts,
held on days perhaps a week or a fortnight apart. This system has
been used in most elections in France since the war. In the first ballot,
anybody may stand; if nobody gets more than 50 per cent of the
votes cast, there has to be a second ballot, in which the less successful
candidates the first time round usually withdraw and urge their
supporters to vote for one or another of the leading contenders.
This system gives everybody a chance of expressing an opinion on
the front runners, even if voters' first preferences are for other
candidates. A variant of it was used in the contest for the Conservative leadership in 1975. The first ballot was essentially between
Edward Heath and Margaret Thatcher, with one minor candidate
also appearing. After winning the first ballot, Mrs. Thatcher pro-
ceeded to another; Heath withdrew and Mrs Thatcher faced and
defeated William Whitelaw and a new trio of minor candidates
who had not stood in the first round.

The AV system would have similar effects to the second ballot.
Voters, instead of marking their ballot papers with a cross, would be
asked to list candidates 1, 2, 3 and so on, in order of preference. If no
candidate got over 50 per cent of the first preferences, the lowest
candidate would be eliminated. His second preferences would then
be allocated, and another count would take place. If there was still
no candidate with an outright majority, the lowest candidate would

again be eliminated, and so on until somebody did get an overall majority. AV was almost introduced in 1931, by the then Labour government which depended on Liberal support, but the proposal was swamped by the political and economic crisis that year which brought down the government. It is used today for elections to the lower house of the Australian parliament.

Two main objections have been raised against AV or second ballot. They come from different standpoints and may even seem to contradict each other, but in fact both are valid. Firstly, these systems are no use to a party that cannot achieve at least second place in the first ballot, or the count of first preferences. If the Liberals were everybody's *second* choice, this alone would do them no good under these systems. They must be the *first* choice of substantial numbers before they can benefit. But secondly, it has been objected that AV would be *too* generous to some minority groups. This may sound odd; but consider the position of the Scottish National Party in October 1974, for example. They came second to Labour and beat the Conservatives, taking Scotland as a whole; the seats they won were mostly taken from the Conservatives. But the majority of Scottish seats are strongly Labour, and these the SNP did not win, though they pushed the Conservatives into third place in most of them. In such seats under AV, the Conservatives would then be eliminated. Almost certainly Tory supporters' second preferences would go to the SNP rather than to Labour, and the SNP would thus win a large number of seats on the second count. As it was they were underrepresented, with 30 per cent of the votes and 15 per cent of the seats. But under AV, that 30 per cent of the votes might well have got them thirty-five or forty seats (over 50 per cent of the total) and they could be strongly *over*represented.

A collection of "fair" results at constituency level does not necessarily lead to a fair result nationwide. This is why supporters of proportional representation (or PR) prefer systems which abandon single-member constituencies. The bigger the constituency, the less likelihood there is that minorities will be unfairly treated. Suppose a party gets 35 per cent of the vote, evenly spread across the whole country: it cannot get 35 per cent of an MP in each single-member constituency, but it can get 35 per cent of the representation in each multi-member unit into which the country is divided.

The logical conclusion of this argument is that the whole country should be turned into one constituency. This is how the party list system operates in its purest form, as in Israel. Each party puts up a list of candidates, which may be as long as the number of seats to be filled. Voters then choose not their favourite candidate, but their favourite party, and seats are allocated to parties in the same proportion as the electorate's votes: thus a party with 40 per cent of the poll could fill 40 per cent of the seats in parliament from the top of its list, another party with 20 per cent could fill the next 20 per cent of seats from the top of *its* list, and so on. There are two obvious objections to this system. First, it involves dropping the idea of *local* representation altogether (and therefore, in its pure form it is used only in Israel, a small, new and largely immigrant state whose citizens had no sense of *local* traditional loyalties comparable to their intense *national* consciousness); secondly, it forces voters to select candidates in the order in which the parties have chosen to list them, and gives them no way of showing their feelings about individual candidates whom they particularly like (or loathe). The countries using list systems (which include Holland, Belgium and West Germany) have tried various modifications to get round these difficulties. Probably the most successful is the West German arrangement, where each voter has two entirely separate votes. He uses the first in an ordinary first-past-the-post election for the single-member territorial constituency in which he lives. With the second, he chooses a party from among all those who have put up candidates in his region. When the votes are counted, every party which has got more than 5 per cent of the total vote is given seats from the list so that the *overall* distribution of seats is strictly proportional to the party votes cast. Thus the system combines proportionality and single-member constituencies. A recent report from the Hansard Society came out in favour of a variant, which they call the additional member system (AMS). In their proposal, only a quarter of the seats would be "additional", compared to half in Germany: this sacrifices some proportionality in order to reduce the size of constituency that the German system would require.

Single transferable vote at work

The other system favoured by reformers is called single transferable vote (STV), and is used in the Republic of Ireland. Under STV, Britain would be divided into multi-member constituencies (probably returning between three and five members each). Each party could put up as many candidates as there were seats to be filled, and the major parties would no doubt do so, while minor parties and stray Independents would be represented by one or two candidates in each constituency. As with AV, voters would be asked to rank the candidates. If there were, say, nine names on the ballot paper, voters would be asked to list them in order of preference from 1 to 9. They would thus have to discriminate not only between parties, but among rival candidates of the same party. The method of counting votes in an STV election depends on the concept of the "quota". This may be defined as the smallest number of votes required to ensure that exactly the right number of candidates is elected. In a four-member seat, for instance, the quota is one-fifth of the first preference votes, plus one; in a five-member seat it is one-sixth of the first preference votes, plus one; generally, in an n-member seat in which P votes have been cast, it is $\frac{P}{n+1} + 1$. To see why this formula is used, consider again the four-member seat. If the quota were exactly one-fifth of the votes cast, then conceivably five candidates could tie, with the same number of votes each. This would result in one candidate too many being elected. The quota is therefore set at the lowest figure which ensures that enough, but not too many, candidates will be successful.

At the first count, voters' first preferences are added up, and any candidate who has achieved more than the quota is declared elected. Such candidates' surplus votes – those above the quota – are then redistributed according to the second preferences shown on them, and so on until nobody else can reach the quota this way. Candidates at the bottom are then eliminated (as in AV) and their second preferences redistributed, and by successive eliminations and re-distributions of surpluses the counting goes on until the correct number of candidates is elected.

Students are often baffled by the arithmetical complexities of STV (they may or may not be helped by the simplified example given in the Appendix, pp. 97–98). But how it works is relatively trivial; it is what it achieves that matters. And here we face many and varied arguments. There are empirical arguments such as: do different electoral systems result in different patterns of party size and strength? And there are questions of values, such as: is it right that we should try to get a more representative electoral system, regardless of the consequences? It seems sensible to discuss these arguments in that order.

Some twenty years ago, a leading French political scientist, Maurice Duverger, pointed to a close relationship which existed between the party system in a given democracy and the electoral system it used to select MPs. After studying voting systems and party alignments in a wide range of democracies, Duverger[1] concluded: "The simple-majority single-ballot system favours the two-party system; the simple-majority system with second ballot and proportional representation favour multi-partyism." This has been generally true. Britain, the United States, Canada and New Zealand all have first-past-the-post electoral systems, and all, broadly speaking, have two-party systems. On the other hand, most continental European democracies use forms of PR, as does the Republic of Ireland. In the great majority of these states there are many small political parties, and most governments take the form of coalitions of several parties.

A little reflection will make it clear why this is so. First-past-the-post systems put a premium on loyalty to the party; PR (especially STV) makes it much easier for individuals or groups to split off and go their own way. In Britain, for instance, an MP who rebels from his party may well be committing political suicide, because at his next election he will be challenged by an official standard-bearer for the party with which he has quarrelled, and only one of the two (at most) can win such a contest. In most parliaments since the war, there have been one or two Conservative or Labour MPs who have rebelled from, or been expelled by, their parliamentary party, and have stood against an official party candidate. (This also happens, rather more often, in local elections.) Until recently, every such candidate has been annihilated by his official opponent. In the early 1970s, there were three cases of Labour MPs in dispute with their local parties who stood against official candidates and won: S. O. Davies in Merthyr, Dick Taverne in Lincoln, and Eddie Milne in Blyth. But Davies died soon after his election, and Taverne and Milne were both defeated in October 1974. In Blyth and Lincoln electors were forced to make the blunt choice between the party and the rebel. Under PR, habitual Labour voters could have indicated a

[1] M. Duverger *Political Parties*, Methuen, 1964, pp. 217, 239.

preference for the rebel without wholly abandoning the party (or vice versa). Election results in the Republic of Ireland show that party rebels do much better under STV than under first-past-the-post. And the same is true of rebel groups and splinter parties. In early 1975, for instance, the Labour Party was badly divided, especially during the EEC Referendum campaign – into pro-Marketeers and anti-Marketeers; militant "Tribune" and right-wing "Manifesto" group members. But all these unfraternal factions were held together (at least for the time being) by one thing: the knowledge that if their party warfare was carried to the polling booth, a split Labour vote would let the Conservatives in and both sides would be the losers. Thus the first-past-the-post formula is a powerful stimulus to party cohesion, and PR encourages differences to be aired in front of the electorate. Under STV, for instance, left-wing and right-wing Labour MPs might not be afraid to split into two parties.

Some commentators have interpreted Duverger as arguing that electoral systems are a *cause* of different party systems: that where there is PR the outcome is a fragmented party system, and where there is a first-past-the-post system the outcome is dominance by two large parties. But this is probably to take the argument too far. Admittedly, governments have sometimes deliberately changed an electoral system in order to get a more favourable distribution of parties. In the Government of Ireland Act of 1920, for instance, the British government of the day stipulated that elections to the Northern Ireland Parliament must be by STV, in order to protect the Catholic minority and ensure that it got its fair share of seats. But what was a fair share in British (and Catholic) eyes was too much for the ruling Protestant Unionist regime, which abolished PR in Northern Ireland in 1929. It was reinstated, for the same reason as it had been first imposed, by the British government in 1973, and did produce a more representative assembly (though this was a hollow triumph, for reasons which will be explained later). However, it is not usually the electoral system, but far more deeply rooted factors, which determine how many parties emerge in any regime. It all depends, to use political scientists' jargon, on the nature of the *cleavages* in the society in question. By "cleavages" are meant things such as class, race and religion, which cause social divisions – usually deepseated and persistent ones. The more cleavages there are in any regime the less likely it is that one party can gain, unassisted, the support of the majority of the electorate.

Different patterns of cleavages have a profound effect on the party system. British politics, for instance, is mainly organised around one cleavage, that of class. Most working-class people vote Labour and most middle-class people vote Conservative. No other division approaches this in importance. Differences of religion, age and sex all have an effect on the basic class cleavage, but it is only a marginal effect. But in Northern Ireland, as everybody knows, things are different. Here class has almost vanished as a political cleavage. Obviously, the main division is religious – between Protestants and Catholics. But across this runs a most important subsidiary division, what might be called "constitutionalist" versus "paramilitary". On one side are parties like the Social Democratic and Labour Party who are not prepared to use violence to achieve their objectives; on the other side groups like the IRA who are.[1] These two cross-cutting cleavages therefore split Northern Irish politicians into four camps, thus:

Protestant constitutionalist	Catholic constitutionalist
Protestant paramilitary	Catholic paramilitary

Individual politicians, and even whole parties, may shift around among these categories, but broadly speaking the "moderate" Unionists and the Alliance Party are "Protestant constitutionalists"; the SDLP is "Catholic constitutionalist"; all the "Loyalist" factions are "Protestant paramilitary" and all factions of the IRA are "Catholic paramilitary". With a different pattern of cleavages, Northern Ireland has a very different party system from the rest of the UK, and the differences were highlighted when the British Government introduced PR using the single transferable

[1] For a fuller discussion of Northern Ireland party politics, see chapter 4, pp. 52–3. Readers unfamiliar with Northern Ireland politics should read that section first.

vote for the elections to the Northern Ireland Assembly in June 1973. After a period of direct rule of Northern Ireland from Westminster, Britain was trying to set up a power-sharing executive: that is, a Northern Irish government which accepted the principle of power shared between Protestant and Catholic representatives. The difficulty was that a large number of Ulster voters and politicians (broadly speaking, those· on what we have called the paramilitary side) wanted no truck with power-sharing. Under first-past-the-post elections their representatives, especially the Protestant "Loyalists", would have done disproportionately well, making the idea of a power-sharing executive unworkable. So the British Government introduced PR with the deliberate intention of protecting minority rights and enhancing the chances of candidates in favour of power-sharing. Besides playing this card twice in Northern Ireland, a British Government has also used it once elsewhere: in Guyana (then the colony of British Guiana) in 1963, when STV was introduced to give a stronger voice to the minority (and more pro-British) party.

The effect of introducing STV in Ulster was just what might have been predicted. The Catholics, with a quarter of the seats in the Assembly, came rather closer to their "fair share" of representation than they had ever done in the first-past-the-post elections to the previous Northern Ireland parliament. But of the three consequences of the change, this was the least significant. Two others bulked larger. First, the Unionist party split down the middle into its constitutionalist and paramilitary factions, thus neatly illustrating Duverger's point. The old Unionist party had contained both moderates and militants, but it had not split for fear of letting in the common enemy. When PR was introduced that constraint was removed. The party no longer had to hold together to avoid letting the enemy in, and it split along the line of cleavage. Secondly – perhaps the most interesting point of all – the new system benefited moderates and harmed extremists. To see why, let us look again at the fourfold division of Ulster political opinion, and enquire in what order each group could be expected to list the rival factions on the ballot paper. Supporters of every faction would presumably put their own first. But the interesting question is: whom would each group put second? A "moderate" Protestant (cell 1) might well put a "moderate"

Protestant constitutionalist			Catholic constitutionalist
	1	2	
Protestant paramilitary	3	4	Catholic paramilitary

Catholic (cell 2) before an extreme Protestant, and a "moderate" Catholic might return the compliment. But supporters of the "extreme" parties on each side do not really have the same freedom of choice. IRA supporters (numerically very few) and "Loyalists" (very numerous) would presumably have to put the "moderates" of their own side second on the ballot. But all IRA candidates (where they stood at all) were eliminated early on, and many Loyalist candidates were elected with large surpluses. In both cases the second preferences of their supporters were taken into account, and a large number of "moderate" candidates were elected, sometimes on the eighth, ninth or tenth count. These candidates would never have been elected at all under any other electoral system.

This triumph of moderation assisted by STV was shortlived. The United Kingdom election of February 1974, fought on conventional lines, gave the Loyalists eleven out of the twelve Northern Ireland seats with 52 per cent of the votes, and the Northern Ireland Assembly collapsed after the Loyalist-led Ulster Workers' Council strike of May 1974, called to demand the ending of the power-sharing assembly. Nevertheless, the experience of the Northern Ireland Assembly teaches us important lessons about what happens in practice when PR is introduced. The bias towards the moderates which was shown would almost certainly work to the advantage of the Liberals if STV were introduced in Britain; relatively speaking, however, the Scottish and Welsh Nationalists stand to gain less from it, as they do not do so badly out of the present system.

One more small point about the impact of STV should be noted: the way in which it forces candidates of the same party to campaign against each other. If there are (say) three seats at stake, each major party will put up three candidates. But hardly any constituencies under STV will be so safe that all three seats would go to the same party. So each candidate who wants to be elected must not only fight the other parties; he must also persuade supporters of his own party to place him, and not his party colleagues, at the head of the ballot. But how is he to do this? He cannot attack his colleagues overtly on policy issues; after all, they are all supposed to support the same objectives. Elections under STV in the Republic of Ireland show what politicians do to get round this problem.

The best way is to be, or to have been, a hero. Irish politicians set a great deal of store by their role (or failing that, their fathers') in the fight for Irish independence between 1916 and 1922. Even today, it is suspiciously easy to find people who were shoulder to shoulder with Padraic Pearse in the GPO during the Easter Rising of 1916. For those who cannot manage this, the next best qualification is prowess on the sports field: Jack Lynch, twice prime minister, rose to fame on the strength of his playing for Cork in the Irish county hurling championships. The value of qualifications like these is that, although not related to party politics, they help to distinguish different candidates of the same party and push the fortunate ones to the head of the ballot. But the candidate who cannot make any of these claims to fame has to find some other way of fighting against his party colleagues, and the commonest way is to outdo them in his assiduousness at promoting and protecting the interests of his constituents. Up to a point, this is admirable; but the Irish experience suggests that MPs in this position may go too far. If a politician spends all his time ensuring that *his* constituents get a new school or a new road or jobs in the civil service, he is not helping in the job of government, which is surely (among much else) to decide where roads and schools are most needed and what national priorities ought to be. It is surely as unsatisfactory if MPs spend too much time promoting their constituents' interests as if they spend too little. One side-effect of STV is to force MPs and candidates into doing just this in order to make sure that they beat their own party colleagues to the head of the poll at the next election.

Should the system be changed?

This is only one small argument in the great debate: is electoral reform a good thing or not? The reader who has got this far may wonder if the question is worth asking. Surely the present electoral system is so self-evidently unfair that nothing except the vested interests of politicians could possibly stand in the way of electoral reform? But there *are* arguments against electoral reform which go beyond pure self-interest, and we ought to consider them. Two points which are commonly made relate to the size of electoral districts under PR. Since STV involves at least three-member seats, constituencies would have to become at least three times as large as they are now (unless the number of MPs was trebled, which is scarcely practicable). The scope for local contact between an MP and his constituents might be reduced. This would be a particular problem in rural areas, especially thinly populated ones like mid-Wales or the Scottish Highlands and Islands. If Scotland north of Inverness became one three-member seat instead of the present three single-member seats, candidates would have to cover some 12,000 square miles of mainland, to say nothing of the far-flung Orkneys and Shetlands. With multi-member seats, by-elections are also a problem, as it is very hard to devise a fair way of running them. Suppose the city of Sheffield became one six-member seat under STV: as it is a strongly working-class, Labour-voting city we might expect Labour to take about four seats and the Conservatives two. But what if one of the Conservatives resigns or dies? However the subsequent by-election is arranged, it is difficult to see how anything other than a Labour victory could result.

But these are minor points. Opponents of PR always base their main argument on the question: what are elections for? Up to now in this chapter, we have looked at electoral systems only to see whether they produce an assembly which is a fair representation, an accurate mirror of the voting patterns of the electorate. But, it is argued, this is not the only purpose, or even the main purpose, of an election. A fairly sophisticated defence of the present electoral system might run somewhat as follows. "Elections are held to produce governments which are capable of running the country, and the best electoral system is the one which is most likely to produce a decisive result. The great virtue of the two-party, first-past-the-post system from this point of view is that it produces clear results. British general elections usually result in a single-party administration with an overall majority, which can get on with the job of governing the country without having to make pacts and deals with other parties. By contrast, PR systems are likely to produce multi-party muddle. Since no one party can produce a parliamentary majority on its own, there will have to be a deal on the floor of parliament between various parties as to who will form a coalition, and what items on each party's programme will have to be dropped in order to satisfy its coalition partners. This has two undesirable consequences. First, it leads to long and frequent ministerial crises during which the country has no effective government because the politicians are trying unavailingly to build a coalition that will have majority support. Second, it means that the voter does not know what sort of government he will get if he votes for a given party. For instance, a Frenchman who voted for the prewar Radical party, in the centre of the political spectrum, might equally well find himself ruled by a right-wing coalition of Radicals and Conservatives, or a left-wing coalition of Radicals and Socialists. Presumably he would rather have had one of these alternatives than the other, but under a multi-party system he would have been given no opportunity to choose."

So runs the case against PR. Elections are held to choose governments; PR encourages multi-partism and hence instability; therefore PR is a bad thing. But even under first-past-the-post, elections where no party gets an overall majority are commoner than many people think. It happened in 1910 (twice), 1923, 1929, and February 1974. Another three elections (1950, 1964 and October 1974) each gave the winning Labour party over 50 per cent but less than 51 per cent of the seats. Thus eight out of 21 General Elections this century failed to guarantee any party a working majority.

As a matter of fact, the whole debate is based on a series of misunderstandings. It is not the electoral system that is at the root of the matter, but the nature of the political cleavages in the society. PR may tend to bring out the effect of the cleavages, and first-past-the-post may tend to conceal them; but they do not create them. In Britain the single dominant cleavage of class has produced a two-party system; but recent elections, paradoxically, have seen a *decline* in class voting[1] (although they were fought on strongly class-related issues), and a rise in voting along other lines than class, especially Scottish nationality and Ulster religion. In France, on the other hand, the tendency has been the other way. Before the war, a multitude of cleavages divided the parties up: peasants against towndwellers, Catholics against anticlerical voters, Communist workers against anti-Communist. Recently, the Gaullist party has been gathering together all the forces on one side, as these old battles fade into the past, while

[1] See chapter 4.

the united Socialist party has been gathering together the forces on the other. In both Britain and France, changes in the number of parties are the result more of changes in the patterns of political cleavage than of different electoral systems. In spite of her second-ballot system, France is changing from a multi-party to a two-party arrangement; in spite of first-past-the-post, Britain is evolving from a two-party to a multi-party system. PR is not very important in the dispute about stable government. If one party can get enough votes to run a government unaided it will do so; if it cannot there must be either a minority government or a coalition. Although the electoral system has an impact on these events it is not at the root of them.

One further point: every political system must cater for a wide range of opinion. If there are 35 million voters in Britain today, there could be up to 35 million opinions as to how the country should be run. But there is only one government, which has to decide how the country *will* be run. Democratic institutions try to ensure that the government's decision in some way reflect what the voters want, but many voters are bound to be unhappy at the outcome – not just supporters of the losing party, but adherents of the winning party who do not approve of what it is doing in power. The problem is exactly the same in every democracy, be it two-party or multi-party; STV, first-past-the-post, second-ballot, or what you will. Everywhere there must be some way of aggregating opinions – that is, of getting from the wide range of conflicting views held by the electorate to the single policy which a government must put into operation. This means that every system depends on coalitions, where people of differing opinions get together for mutual advantage. In a two-party system, the coalitions are commonly within parties. The Labour and Conservative Parties are both many-sided coalitions (as indeed is the Liberal Party). All incorporate people with conflicting views who are held together by the knowledge that they must present a united front at election time, to avoid the risk of the other side getting in. In a multi-party system, parties are ideologically purer; they do not cover nearly so wide a range of opinions as (say) the British Labour Party. But this does not remove the need for coalition building, it merely shifts it. Instead of bargains and compromises being struck *within* parties, they have to be made *between* them, on the floor of the assembly. In the British system as it has existed so far, we have had strong disciplined parties, able to form stable administrations, but at a cost: that parties would often have to ignore the views of large numbers of their fervent supporters in order to carry out the business of government. If (perhaps helped by a change in the voting system) Britain developed multi-party politics, parties could be more faithful to their supporters, if they wished, but at a cost: the permanent exclusion from government of anybody unwilling to take part in the process of bargaining and coalition-building. In the last analysis, the question of principle we have been discussing – whether we ought to have electoral reform or not – is really much less important than those on both sides of the argument think. PR of itself would not bring about the break-up of the British party system; and if the system did change, this would only imply that some political decision-making had shifted from one place to another.

Throughout this chapter I have spoken freely of the views and opinions of parties *and* of their supporters. But readers should not assume that the two are necessarily the same: that people who vote for, or people who do voluntary work for, a party necessarily hold the same views about politics as the leaders of that party. This is one of the main themes of chapter 3.

3 Are Voters Rational?

The fear of irrational voting

As long as democracy has existed it has had trenchant critics. One recurring argument has been that people simply do not know their own best interests: they have not the intellectual equipment to make a democratic choice. In a word, voters are irrational.

There is some fragmentary evidence to support this attack, even in its extreme form. For instance, one rather alarming thing has been noticed about voting in some British elections, especially local elections. In some local elections more than one vacancy occurs, so that voters have as many votes as there are places to be filled. If this happens the major parties will usually each put up a full slate of candidates, and interesting comparisons can be made between the performance of different candidates of the same party. And the message is clear: the candidates who do best are those whose surnames are near the beginning of the alphabet, and who therefore appear at the head of the ballot. This happens too regularly to be mere coincidence, and it shows that a number of voters are simply plumping for the first name on the ballot paper, irrespective of party. This can hardly be called rational voting behaviour, however much it may benefit politicians whose names begin with the letter A.[1] Indeed, if Britain changed over to STV or another of the electoral systems discussed in chapter 2 which demand multi-member constituencies, this alphabetical bias would almost certainly become more noticeable.

But nobody claims that very many voters behave in this entirely

---

[1] Interested readers may wish to look up the list of British prime ministers since (say) 1900 in any reference book, where they may discover some interesting facts about prime ministers' surnames.

irrational way. Over the years the attack on voters' rationality has usually taken different forms, but in one form or another the arguments are very ancient. One of the first, and most vehement, critics of democracy was Plato, who wrote in Athens 2,500 years ago. Many Athenians had been proud of their democratic system of government but Plato thought the outcome had been a series of ignorant demagogues, men who were good at whipping up popular emotions but incapable of governing the state. He compared the citizens of Athens to the crew of a ship who are given the chance of electing their captain. The man best fitted for the job is the man who has spent years studying seamanship, navigation and astronomy. But the crew prefer the orator who makes them the most extravagant promises about his ability to navigate, and they dismiss the true navigator as an idle star-gazer. So they vote for the orator, who takes command, with the result that the ship is driven on to the rocks and wrecked.

After the decline of democracy in ancient Greece, it was out of favour as a system of government until relatively modern times. But as democracy revived, so did doubts about voters' ability to live up to it, even among some fervent advocates of democracy. One of these was John Stuart Mill, the famous nineteenth-century prophet of liberalism. Mill was a democrat; he advocated a widening of the franchise, and the granting of votes to women (who did not get them until 1918). But he was worried about some of the consequences of democracy. Would it lead to the suppression of individuality and initiative in favour of a desire for uniformity? And would it mean that the numerical majority of the ill-informed and uneducated should have enough votes to swamp the considered opinions of educated men?

More than one criticism of democracy lay behind fears like these. There was the argument that voters were easily misled by plausible politicians, and the (rather separate) concern that the majority might ignore or actively stifle the wishes of minorities. The second point raises some awkward questions of principle, which are considered in chapter 6. But the first point should be investigated now: how vulnerable is democracy to the ill-considered or irrational votes and opinions of a mass electorate?

In the nineteenth century it was intellectually respectable to disapprove of democracy; in the twentieth century it is not, and

Mill's worries about the ability of the electorate to sustain democracy have been rather pushed to one side until recently. In any case, it was not until the techniques of survey research were developed, starting in the late 1930s, that any valid generalisations could be made about such things as voters' appreciation of, and attitudes to, political issues. It was shortly after the Second World War that American and British researchers who had been studying voting behaviour were first able to come to conclusions about the rationality of the mass electorate. They started out by assuming that voters would make "rational choices" like those an economist supposes would be made by an intelligent purchaser choosing a new car. Which party, according to its manifesto, has a bundle of policies which is closest to the range of things I want? Which party has the best record of reliability, for carrying out its promises once it is in power? Questions like these, the early researchers assumed, were what intelligent voters should be asking themselves before they decided which way to cast their votes.

Survey research and rationality

A good example of these investigations was a survey made of public opinion in Greenwich at the general election in 1950. To understand its findings we must say something about the main political controversies of those far-off days. In February 1950 the Labour Government of Clement Attlee faced the country at the end of the first ever Labour administration to have a clear parliamentary majority. Attlee's government had had mixed fortunes. It had carried out almost all of its commitment to nationalise the basic industries and services in Britain – coal, transport, gas, electricity, the Bank of England – and had created the National Health Service and the Welfare State. These were monumental achievements. But it had been dogged by austerity and shortages. Rationing of food, fuel and petrol was still almost as intense as at the end of the Second World War. There had been a severe fuel crisis in 1947, when a hard winter had brought transport of fuel almost to a halt. Overseas, the outstanding political fact was the dropping of the "iron curtain": that is to say, the freezing of relations between the wartime Western allies and Soviet Russia, and the setting up of Soviet-dominated Communist regimes in all the states of Eastern Europe. In the election campaign of 1950 the Conservatives bitterly attacked nationalisation and rationing, and warned that Socialism was a dangerous stepping-stone to Communism. They were also against any dismantling of the British Empire. In 1950 India had just been given its independence, and the Conservatives wanted Britain to hold on to her remaining colonies in Africa and Asia. The Labour campaign, on the other hand, was essentially a defence of the outgoing government's record, and especially its achievement in maintaining full employment after the end of the war.

The researchers at Greenwich picked a number of policy statements from the opposing manifestoes of the two main parties which dealt with the political questions of the day. They then tested the statements out on political activists to make sure that they recognised them for what they were and assigned them to the right party. Next, the statements were put to a sample drawn from the electorate of Greenwich. The results were startling. More than half of the Labour voters in the sample agreed with a number of statements of Conservative policy, no less than 65 per cent of them agreeing that "Foreign policy should be based on 'Empire First'". Contrariwise a substantial number of Conservative supporters agreed with Labour propositions such as "Goverment planning is essential for full employment". Twenty-one per cent of the Labour voters and 7 per cent of the Conservatives actually agreed with more of the opposite party's policies than of their own party's. A large number of voters were behaving in a way which, on the face of it, seemed highly irrational.

At the same time, research was being done in Britain and America on how much voters knew about politics and how likely they were to change their votes. Elections results obviously depended on floating voters, who changed their vote from one election to the next: but who were the floating voters? It was assumed that most of them came from the most highly educated and best informed sections of the electorate. The mental picture was of two large blocks of voters habitually and without much thought giving their votes to the two main parties, and in the middle a group of rational men weighing up the merits of the parties in the way J. S. Mill hoped that responsible citizens would do. To the chagrin of the researchers they found the opposite. The best informed voters were mostly among those who had the firmest and most unshakable convictions, and whose party choice was least likely to deviate during the course of an election campaign. The typical floating voter, on the other hand, was found to be somebody who was not very interested in politics, and who did not know very much about the parties and issues involved. This was a long way away from the image of the rational sceptic envisaged by Mill and some of his successors. The first modern voting study was made at the time of the American presidential election of 1940; but publication of the results was actually held up for a year because the results of the research were so different from what had been expected. Instead of finding rational choices of the sort just described, those making the survey had found instead a picture of voting which seemed to be dependent on habit, custom, or sheer ignorance.

A reader of these voting studies comes away with the distinct impression that the electorate is being severely ticked off for not trying. Its level of political information is low, and its political beliefs are incoherent. "Could try harder" is written all over the headmaster's report. In particular, the relationship between people's beliefs and their choice of party is the opposite of what was expected. Instead of choosing a party on the strength of their beliefs, it appeared that many voters chose their beliefs on the strength of their party allegiance. That is to say, they had no opinion at all on many issues until the party they favoured took a firm stand, whereupon they would fall into line behind their party. This helps to explain the otherwise curious finding that voters' opinions on issues fluctuate more widely and more often than their opinions on which party they support. There are two clear examples of this relationship in recent British politics: the European Common Market (the EEC) and the question of incomes policy or wage restraint.

Britain's first unsuccessful application to join the EEC was made by the Conservative government in 1961, and opposed by the Labour Party. Soon after Labour came into office in 1964, however, its leaders decided that the Common Market was a good thing after all. Therefore the Labour government applied to join, again unsuccessfully, in 1967. After 1970 the scene changed again. The new Conservative government was in favour of entry, and Labour was once again opposed to it. Supporters of both sides throughout made great play of the state of public opinion, and the public opinion polls indeed gave results so confused that both sides could often draw comfort from them, sometimes simultaneously. The proportion of the British public which was in favour of entry fluctuated very widely, and the figures seem to have no pattern at all, until they are related to party choice. Then it becomes clear that voters tended to have the same opinion about the EEC as the party of their choice, so that, for instance, Labour supporters tended to be anti-Market in 1961, pro-Market in 1967, and anti-Market again in 1971. Their opinions on the Market were not *causes* of their party choice, but *consequences* of it. A similar story can be told about attitudes to incomes policy. The Labour Party was for incomes policy in 1969, and against it from 1970 to 1974. In 1974 the Labour leaders pinned their faith in a "Social Contract" with the trades unions on a voluntary basis, but by 1975 they had returned to the idea of a statutory wages policy. The Conservative leaders were strongly against incomes policies up to about 1972, and then equally strongly in favour. Most opinion polls show the electorate to be more widely in favour of incomes policies than politicians are; but the interesting point is that Labour voters favoured them most when the Labour Party in parliament did, and similarly with Conservative voters.

But are the voters so stupid?

This is the sort of finding which drew schoolmasterly rebukes from the American analysts because it appeared to show that the electorate was behaving irrationally. However, two very important points should be made in the electorate's defence.

The first concerns what have been called "belief systems" or ideologies. These are sets of political beliefs ranging over more than one issue. Many politicians and others interested in politics have wide-ranging ideologies which shape their views on all sorts of political questions. To take a particularly clear example, Marxists believe that all politics (and much else besides) is an expression of class conflict, and in particular of conflict between bourgeoisie and proletariat, between middle-class and working-class. Therefore in domestic politics a Marxist would support all efforts by wage-earners to get higher wages, while in foreign affairs he will attack imperialism and colonialism, which he sees as oppression of the workers in overseas territories by capitalist powers like Britain and the USA. He thus has an ideology which links his views on domestic and foreign policy. There may not seem to be any connection between industrial relations and (say) the Vietnam war, but Marxist ideology links them together.

Most politicians have some sort of belief system to organise their views on different issues. It may not be so rigorous as the Marxist's, but it is undoubtedly present, and it enables politicians and commentators to talk a common language and identify each other's views. The distinction most often used is between left and right, or between liberal and conservative. There is a bundle of beliefs that is recognised as characteristically left-wing, and another which is seen as right-wing or conservative. If I say that a British politician is left-wing, I imply that he has a number of diverse beliefs. He supports the public ownership of industry; he favours generous social welfare benefits; he probably approves of "the permissive society" and thinks that people's moral and sexual behaviour is their own business; he is opposed to undemocratic regimes in places like Spain, Chile and South Africa and would like to see majority rule in Rhodesia (but probably not in Northern Ireland). Similarly, if I call a politician right-wing I mean that he holds opposite views on most or all of diverse questions like these.

Political comment in the newspapers and television is full of the terms "left" and "right", "liberal" and "conservative". To those who know what they connote, they can be convenient shorthand terms, and they are used as such elsewhere in this book. But one consistent finding of the voting surveys, both British and American, is that the mass electorate does not think in these terms, and often cannot attach any meaning at all to words like "left" and "right". On the most generous interpretation, no more than 40 per cent of the British electorate has any understanding of these terms in the way they are used by politicians and journalists.

This may look like still further evidence of the irredeemable stupidity of the electorate. But is it fair to argue in this way? The electorate is under no obligation to think in the same terms as politicians. There is no *logical* reason why support for the public ownership of industry should go along with (say) belief in the permissive society. In fact, the reasons are mostly historical, as we may see if we pursue this example a little further. The Labour Party is a coalition of diverse pressure groups which were welded together in the years following 1900. One of these groups was the trade union movement, interested in reforms which it hoped would benefit the working class, such as nationalisation of industry; another was the radical liberal movement, largely middle-class in social composition.

This comprised people who took their liberal views from writers such as J. S. Mill, and argued that matters like sexual habits were an individual's private business and should not be enforced by law or even moral coercion. For various reasons, such people drifted from the Liberal Party to the Labour Party in the years between 1900 and 1939. But there is no logically necessary reason why their views should be linked with views about public ownership to form a left-wing belief system. It is simply a historical accident.

The average voter is not so involved in politics as politicians are. This may sound so obvious as to be not worth saying, but it is often ignored. For most people, most of the time, there are other things which are more important to them. It would be eccentric to argue that a man's vote was more important to him than, say, his daughter's wedding. And to be able to share in the ideologies of left-wing or right-wing politics, a man would have to do very much more than vote. He would have to be an assiduous reader of political comment in the newspapers, an avid follower of current affairs on television, even perhaps a regular attender at monthly meetings of the local branch of his political party. For only through a great deal of this sort of activity would an elector be exposed to left and right ideological thinking. Short of this, there would be no way of informing him what sets of beliefs "ought" to go together.

Thus although voters may not link issues together and perceive the stands parties take on them in the same way that political activists do, they are not necessarily being irrational. We must remember that many political issues are very remote from almost every citizen, and the only sensible view for him to have is "no opinion", unless he already has some sort of ideology or belief system which provides him with a more or less readymade opinion on new issues which come to him. There are examples of this in the Greenwich survey of 1950, in which so many voters "failed the examination" of seeing which statements belonged to "their" party. As we have mentioned, 65 per cent of Labour supporters agreed with the Conservative proposition, "Our foreign policy should be based on 'Empire First' ". People immersed in the political issues of the day might find this odd or difficult to understand, but only because they were looking at the question from within a particular belief system which says that support of working-class interests and opposition to the British Empire go together. This is a historically true statement about the British Labour Party; it is in no way a logically necessary one. There is no reason why a voter should not say: "I support Labour because I want full employment in Britain, and I think the Labour Party is most likely to achieve it; I am not very concerned about the British Empire, but I suppose I am for it, whatever the Labour Party's view may be". And if he is not very concerned about the British Empire, it hardly matters that he, as a Labour voter, has not troubled to work out what his view "ought" to be if he adhered to the left–right pattern of thought. The future of the Empire was of great importance to the Labour Colonial Secretary or his Conservative opponent; to white settlers in Kenya or black rebels in Bechuanaland. It was of no importance to the average elector of Greenwich. It seems pointless to expect voters to have opinions about issues in which they are not interested.

Research shows that voters *do* have strong opinions on some questions, although they do not always slot neatly into party ideology. Economic wellbeing dominates all else in most voters' minds. As we shall see in chapter 5, people's day-to-day views about politics are very much affected by their feelings of prosperity or otherwise. But there are other questions on which voters tend to have strong opinions: matters like pensions, industrial relations, race and capital punishment. An investigator who asks voters, "Do you think hanging should be restored?" will get meaningful answers. But if he asks, "Do you approve of NATO?" he may get entirely random answers which have no real meaning at all. Most people have no opinion on NATO, but many may feel that they have to give an answer when asked for one.

Thus it is no disproof of voters' rationality to show that they may vote for a party without supporting it on the full range of issues it endorses, or even without finding out what, in full, the party stands for. This is linked with another point about "rational voting". If a voter really did behave like a calculating machine with a brain, he might very well decide that it was not worth his while to vote at all. Most of us have better things to do with our time than go out on a dark wet night when most of the street lights are out (28 February 1974 was such a night) in order to vote, when we think how unlikely it is that our single votes will make any difference. Most of us live in safe seats; and even if we do not, the chances of ours being the crucial vote which determines the result are very tiny. Anybody who doubts this need only ask himself how often British election contests are won with a majority of one. Besides, each of us has only one vote, in one constituency, but the result of a general election depends on 635 individual contests, so it is unlikely that the result in a single constituency will have a significant part in determining who rules Britain for the next four or five years. Perhaps the only truly rational thing to do is to sit at home in the warm and watch television.

The obvious objection to this is "But what if everybody thought like that?" If everybody thought like that, the whole system would collapse, since nobody would ever vote. Not many of us want to see the system collapse into anarchy (and those who do rarely argue that universal abstention is the way to achieve it). Therefore it may, after all, be perfectly rational to vote in order to keep the system going. This thought seems to correspond to some deepseated feelings among British electors, especially older voters. A local newspaper reporter caught a revealing snatch of conversation between two voters who had just turned out to vote at a municipal election in 1973. "I didn't think you were going to vote." "Neither I was, until I saw that Hitler film on TV last night." Hitler is dead and gone; what relevance could his career have to the choice between Labour and Conservative candidates for the local council? The thought in the voter's mind is surely that it was the collapse of democracy in prewar Germany that produced Hitler; to avoid the risk of the same happening here, we must be sure to cast our votes – whether for Labour, Liberal or Conservative is immaterial. "I was marking my paper, just to make sure," the voter confided to her friend. Just to make sure, not that any particular candidate won, but that the democratic system was kept going.

Reassuring though this argument is, it is not as strong as it looks. For if I am a rational man who sees that it would be disastrous if everybody behaved "rationally" and abstained, I must also see that every other rational man is capable of the same thought process. Since they all, equally, wish to avoid anarchy, it follows that all of *them* will vote to avoid this outcome. Thus the system will be preserved without my efforts, and I still do not have to vote in order to preserve it. But then it may occur to me that everybody else will realise that others will vote to keep the system going, so perhaps after all they *will* abstain. From this point onwards, the argument simply goes round in circles; we cannot know what to expect of our fellow-citizens. This may be an argument for voting in order to save the system from collapse, but it is not a very strong one.

It seems, then, that a truly rational elector would have worked out that, however passionately he was concerned with politics, it would not usually be worth his while to vote, let alone spend time acquiring political information. It is perhaps just as well that voters do not generally act according to this sort of rationality. Besides, as we have said, the "examination" which the voters of the 1950s, in Greenwich and elsewhere, failed was not very fair. Voters failed to link items such as nationalisation and anti-colonialism, which went together in the belief systems of politicians. But nobody has ever suggested any convincing reasons why voters should have to share the belief systems of politicians and journalists. For these reasons, it seems that the fears expressed about the rationality of voters were much exaggerated.

Votes and interests

In any case, the rational voter attacked by these writers was a man of straw. Few serious commentators have ever believed that most voters can or do approach politics as if they were professional politicians. And every enquiry into voting behaviour has found plenty of voters motivated by feelings of group interests, even if not elaborated into a full-blown ideology. The American who dislikes Negroes and therefore votes Republican because the Democrats are the party of the Blacks, or the British working man who supports Labour because he sees Labour as being the party of the working class, are surely behaving in a perfectly rational way.

Traditionally, most of the British electorate has had an inbuilt, habitual allegiance to one party. This may be changing in the volatile 1970s, but up till now the pattern has been clear. Most working-class people vote Labour, though enough of them vote Conservative to ensure that the Labour Party is by no means always in power; most middle-class people vote Conservative, though the few who vote Labour form a highly visible section of the population and are often important within the Labour Party. These relationships are examined more closely in chapters 4 and 5. For now, the important point is the rationality of habitual allegiance. Is it rational for me to vote for (say) the Labour Party, when it is committed to doing some things I disapprove of, such as dismantling the British Empire?

This question has already been partly answered, but other points can be made. To identify Labour with working-class interests and the Conservatives with middle-class ones is not stupid, nor haphazard. It would not be equally sensible to argue that the connection should be the other way. Of course, every party will claim to represent the whole people. But the parties are, historically, coalitions of pressure groups representing different interests. The Labour Party could not have existed in its present form without the trade unions. Up to 1900 most trade union leaders voted Liberal, and advised their members to do likewise. Then came the shock of the Taff Vale case, and things were never the same again. In September 1900 the courts ruled that the Taff Vale Railway Company was entitled to sue the railwaymen's union for the losses arising out of a strike on that railway. This decision threatened the very existence of trade unions, since every time their members struck they might become liable to pay heavy damages. So the union leaders transferred their support from the Liberal Party to a new body called the Labour Representation Committee, whose object was to return MPs to parliament to speak for working-class interests, such as the reversal of the Taff Vale decision. In 1906 this body retitled itself the Labour Party, as it has remained ever since. Thus there is an obvious historical reason for saying that Labour represents working-class interests. Likewise, the Conservative Party is a coalition in which the interests of business and agriculture have long been prominent. In the nineteenth century the Liberals were the businessmen's party, but from about the beginning of the twentieth century businessmen turned to the Conservatives instead. The Conservatives are unmistakably the party of the middle-class.

It is easy to argue, for instance, that Labour does not *really* represent working-class interests; indeed this is said both by left-wingers who think Labour is not doing enough to end capitalism and by right-wingers who think Labour is too subservient to powerful trade unions. But it may still be right for a voter to ignore views like these, and vote as he has always done. For an important point about choice at a general election is that the voter is not being asked to compare like with like. One party has just been in office, and can be judged on its record; the others have not, and can only be judged on their promises. Promising things is easier than doing them, and it is therefore hard to get a fair comparison. In 1974, for instance, a voter might say, "The Conservatives have made a mess of the economy; Labour promises to do better; therefore I shall vote Labour". But this would not be very wise. He can have no way of knowing how likely the Labour Party is to live up to its promises, unless he draws on past experience. Even the lessons of past experience may be ambiguous, because no government faces the same set of events as its predecessor.

In this situation, a voter is surely justified in falling back on "interest group" ideas – on attitudes such as "Labour is for the working-class", or "the Conservatives have the welfare of small shopkeepers at heart". It could be argued that these are dangerous attitudes: that Labour is by no means always for the working-class, or that the Conservatives often conspicuously fail to cater for the interests of small shopkeepers. But it is difficult to see how this problem can be avoided. A voter has to rely on parties' general records. Their campaign promises tell him very little; and they tell him nothing at all about what the parties will do to meet contingencies that have not yet arisen, but might occur in the future. Custom and habit may be the best guides, after all. And if a voter's party does anything which has sufficient impact on him to make him wish to revoke his habitual support, he can always do so.

There are distinct signs that the force of habit in British elections is weakening. Between 1966 and 1970, when Labour was in office, there were swings of unprecedented size against the Labour Party in by-elections and municipal elections. One of the most remarkable by-elections was in 1968 at Dudley, in the West Midlands, when a Labour majority of 10,000 was converted to a Conservative lead of 11,600, a swing of 21 per cent. At the same time, Scottish Nationalists were making spectacular strides, winning the previously rock-ribbed Labour seat of Hamilton at a by-election in 1967 and getting more votes than any other party at the Scottish municipal elections of 1968.

These results, which are examined more closely in chapter 5, were overshadowed by the 1970 general election, in which Labour recovered most of its lost ground and Liberals and other parties did badly. But the dominance of the two main parties was badly shaken in the elections of 1974. In February the Liberal vote trebled from two million to six million, and dipped again, but only to five million, in October. In February, thirty-seven and in October thirty-nine MPs were elected who were neither Labour nor Conservative – the largest numbers at any election since 1935. Though this number dropped to 27 in 1979, it is still clear that force of habit is weakening, and that electors no longer have such an automatic allegiance to "their" party as they once did. Two particular aspects of the 1974 results give force to this argument: the temporary success of the Labour Independents and the evident increase of strategic voting.

In chapter 2 we mentioned how three former Labour MPs, S. O. Davies, Dick Taverne and Eddie Milne, stood as Independents after being disowned by their local Labour parties, and won. Whether this trend will continue or not remains to be seen. Both Taverne and Milne were defeated in October 1974, and another ex-MP who had likewise fallen out with his local party – Eddie Griffiths in the Brightside division of Sheffield – lost to an official candidate (though he still did better than rebel Independents usually did in the 1950s and 1960s). On the other hand it is clear that local Labour parties are becoming readier to disown sitting MPs whom they disapprove of. The most spectacular case to date is that of Reg Prentice, a Cabinet Minister, whom his local party in Newham North-east decided not to readopt in July 1975 because they disapproved of his forcefully expressed right-wing views. Nothing came of this in the end, however. Prentice crossed the floor of the House and in 1979 was elected Conservative MP for Daventry; Labour regained Newham North East.

Although right-wing Labour MPs like Taverne, Griffiths and Prentice who fall out with militant left-wing local parties provide the commonest cause of these disputes, they are not only about ideology. And, indeed, both Davies and Milne were if anything left-wing rebels. The relative success of the rebels, both left-wing and right-wing, shows that the electorate is looking more to the man and less to the party than previously, especially if the man in question is the sitting MP. It remains to be seen whether the trend will become more widespread, and particularly whether any cases are likely to occur on the Conservative side. But it no longer seems as true as it once was that the electorate would vote for anybody, so long as he was wearing the right party colour.

This is linked with a noticeable increase in strategic voting in recent elections. Voters seem to be becoming much more aware of the situation of the parties in their own constituency, and more ready to desert parties which have no chance of winning in favour of those that have. This was shown in a variety of ways in both general elections during 1974, especially the February election. For instance, the Labour vote in a number of safe Conservative seats, especially in southern England, slumped, whereas the Liberal vote shot up. It is pretty certain that many Labour supporters in such seats were casting strategic votes for the Liberals. Since Labour could not keep the Conservatives out, they would vote instead for a party that might. A striking instance is the Berwick-on-Tweed constituency. This was narrowly won by the Liberals from the Conservatives at a by-election in 1973. Before the February 1974 general election, there were several press reports that Labour voters in the division were going to vote Liberal "to keep the Tories out". This appears to have happened: the Labour vote slumped, with the candidate losing his deposit, while the Liberal vote went up. The Conservative vote rose as well, but the Liberal managed to stay ahead. Similarly, in a number of safe Labour seats in 1974 the Conservative vote dropped while the Liberal share increased.

An allied phenomenon was the dramatic improvement in the votes cast for some MPs from minority parties. Three Liberal MPs who had all scraped in by majorities of under 1,000 in 1970 were returned by majorities ranging from 8,700 to 11,000 in February 1974; and the SNP member for the Western Isles saw his majority rise from 726 (4·8 per cent above his nearest rival) to 7,200 (47·9 per cent). Here again, it seems that many normal supporters of other parties were voting for the sitting MP, often because they thought their party had no chance of winning.

On balance, then, the more extreme claims that voters are irrational are not justifiable. Certainly, voters are not as well informed as some earlier writers expected or hoped. They do not think about politics in politicians' language. But for the most part they vote according to a quite coherent perception of their interests, tempered by a growing appreciation of the strategic position in different constituencies. If this is not rationality, it is surely a close enough approach to satisfy most people.

4 Voting Behaviour: the formation of basic allegiances

Class and party

The most important fact about voting behaviour in Britain is its close connection with social class. The majority of middle-class voters vote Conservative, and of working-class voters vote Labour. In the words of a well-known authority: "Class is the basis of British party politics; all else is embellishment and detail."[1] This may seem so obvious as to be hardly worth saying, but it is in fact something that picks Britain out from other democracies: the class orientation of British politics is almost uniquely strong. Admittedly, class is a factor in the political divisions of almost every democracy, and many countries, including France, Italy, Canada, Australia and New Zealand, have political parties which are distinctively class based. But only in New Zealand and Scandinavia does the intensity of class voting approach the British level. That is to say, only these countries have as few voters who depart from the general pattern of the working-class voting for one party and the middle-class voting for a rival party. From 1945 to 1970 the two big parties established an almost total dominance over British politics. Though their dominance in terms of votes was never so total as in terms of seats in the Commons, they held the allegiance of between 80 and 90 per cent of those who voted.

The following table shows the relationship between class and party as found by the opinion polls in 1970:

[1] P. G. J. Pulzer, *Political Representation and Elections in Britain*, 3rd edn Allen & Unwin, 1975, p. 102.

Table 4.1. *Class and Party, 1970* (%)

Party	Class				
	AB (Managers, administrative professional workers)	C_1 (Junior management, supervisory and clerical workers)	C_2 (Skilled manual workers)	DE (Unskilled manual workers, casual workers, pensioners)	All
Conservative	79	59	35	33	46
Labour	10	30	55	57	44
Liberal	10	9	7	6	8
Others	1	2	3	4	2
	100	100	100	100	100

The letters AB, C_1, C_2 and DE denote the classification usually used by market research and opinion poll organisations. A description of the sort of jobs included in each category is added underneath. Broadly speaking, A, B, and C_1 are regarded as "middle-class", and C_2, D, and E as "working-class".

Source: Adapted from P. G. J. Pulzer, *Political Representation and Elections in Britain*, 3rd edn, Allen & Unwin, 1975, p. 109.

From these figures it will be seen that upper middle-class people [group AB] are the most strongly class-conscious of any in Britain, in the sense that they are more solidly in support of the party which "belongs" to their class than any other group. The Labour majority among working-class voters [classes C_2, D and E], although substantial, is by no means overwhelming. An important minority, about a third, of working-class voters regularly support the Conservatives. If we look at the same statistics from the opposite direction, this means that the Conservatives draw as much as half their support from working-class voters.

This is a very important facet of British voting behaviour. If it were not for the working-class Conservative vote, the Labour Party would be permanently in power. Since there are many more working-class than middle-class voters, if Britain had 100 per cent class voting the working-class party would win every election. Some would welcome this, others deplore it; but at any rate it would produce a political system very *different* from the one which actually exists. It was as long ago as 1867 that a substantial proportion of working-class men first got the vote; and many observers at the time, including Liberals such as John Stuart Mill and Robert Lowe, were alarmed lest the workers should use their voting power to create a monolithic class party which would completely ignore the interests of everybody other than the industrial working-class. But in fact, the Conservatives have been in power, alone or in coalition, for 71 of the 113 years that have passed since the 1867 Reform Act. Only four times in the last century have the Conservatives been out of office for five consecutive years or more: during the Liberal governments of 1880–85 and 1906–15, and the Labour administrations of 1945–51 and 1964–70. Working-class Conservative voters have therefore played a crucial role in the shaping of the modern British party system. They form the most significant single exception to the general rule of class voting, and it is therefore important to investigate why they are so numerous.

One view is that the Conservatives benefit from what has been called the "deference" vote. A substantial minority of working-class voters feel that they ought to support candidates of education and good class – in a word, of "breeding". When asked by two sociologists investigating political attitudes whether they would prefer to have as prime minister an MP's son from Eton and Oxford or a lorry-driver's son from grammar school, many working-class Conservatives plumped for the public school man.

It's something that's ingrained in them. He's been to a good public school and I know a lot of people run them down [but] you can tell breeding. It's ingrained. He's a born leader and I'm not saying that the other one hasn't done well, but he hasn't got that quality in him.[1]

The Conservatives undoubtedly benefit from the "deference" vote in this way. More generally, the Conservative Party profits from its association with national symbols – the Queen, the National Anthem,

[1] R. T. McKenzie and A. Silver, *Angels in Marble*, Heinemann, 1968, p. 168

the Union Jack (which is regarded as so much of a Conservative possession that it appears, in a truncated form, on official party literature). The Conservative Party has always projected itself as the national party, the patriotic party, and has tried to portray the opposition party of the day – the Liberals at the time of the Boer War, the Labour Party at the time of the cold war of the 1950s – as in some sense "unEnglish" or indeed "disloyal". To many working-class voters these symbols have much greater attraction than the appeals of class based politics.

Contrasted with deferential working-class voters are so-called seculars, who vote Conservative simply because they feel that the Conservatives will make a better job of running the country, or benefiting the individual voter, than the Labour Party. There is no reason to suppose that there is a higher proportion of "secular" working-class Conservative supporters than of middle-class voters who cross class lines in the opposite direction to vote Labour, and these two factors would cancel each other out except that, since there are more working-class than middle-class voters altogether, a similar proportion means a higher absolute number.

But overall, there must be more working-class Conservative supporters than middle-class Labour ones – not only in absolute numbers but also in proportionate terms. If this were not so, Labour would win every election, which (as we have seen) is very far from being the case. So there must be further reasons for the working-class Conservative vote. Two further explanations of it, based on detailed survey research, have been put forward. One is that voting behaviour is affected by a voter's political environment. In other words, if I am surrounded at home, at work, or in the pub by Labour-voting friends, I am most likely to conform to the pattern and vote Labour; but if all my social contacts are with Conservative voters, I am much more likely to go their way, regardless of social class. This helps to explain why the Labour vote fluctuates from constituency to constituency far more than does the proportion of manual workers. Two extreme examples are the constituencies of Abertillery and Blackpool South. Abertillery is in the heart of the mining valleys of South Wales, where, after a long and stormy history of class conflict earlier this century, feelings of working-class solidarity are perhaps stronger than anywhere else in Britain. Here, in 1970 84·7 per cent of the electorate comprised manual workers, and 81·4 per cent of the vote went to Labour. The class war has never been acute in Blackpool, however; in Blackpool South, although 65·5 per cent of the electors were working-class, the Labour vote was only 33 per cent of the total. It does not take much imagination to see why; in a totally different environment, all the social pressures which exist in places like Abertillery to encourage people to vote Labour are absent in a town full of seaside landladies. One survey, by Butler and Stokes, found that working-class voters in seaside resorts were actually *more* likely to vote Conservative than Labour. Here, then, is another source of the working-class Conservative vote.

There is another way of looking at the problem, which takes us much further afield and which, unlike the previous explanations, shows why there should be a higher proportion of working-class Conservatives than of middle-class socialists. When voters are divided by age, it is found that the heaviest preponderance of working-class Conservatives is among the oldest voters; with middle-aged and younger voters, the proportion of middle-class Labour supporters is actually higher than that of working-class Conservatives. But the reason for this is *not* the popular belief that people become more conservative as they grow older; it is that when today's elderly voters were young, there was no Labour Party for them to support, and party politics in Britain had not been formed into the class-based mould which it occupies today. People first become aware of political parties in a meaningful way in their adolescent and early adult years, and the impressions then formed exercise a very powerful influence over the political behaviour of many voters all their lives. The electorate still contains a number of voters who grew to adult-hood before the Labour Party became a national challenger for power, and very many more whose parents lived under a different pattern of party competition – in the days when, in W. S. Gilbert's much-quoted words,

Every boy and every girl That's born into this world alive
Is either a little Liberal Or else a little Conservative.

In the Liberal and Conservative Party fights of a century ago can be found the origins of the present class alignment. But politics before 1918 was by no means solely about class; there were other divisions of equal importance, and their influence can still be traced in the electorate of today.

The growth of class alignment since 1867

Many people are familiar with the outlines of British party history since 1867. The alternation of Liberal and Conservative governments was upset by the serious split in the Liberal Party in 1886, when the Liberal Unionists, who were opposed to granting Home Rule to Ireland, seceded and eventually joined the Conservatives; there followed a period of Conservative dominance ended by the great Liberal victory of 1906. Meanwhile the Labour Party had been founded in 1900, essentially as a pressure group to protect the interests of trade unionists; it did not initially challenge the Liberals, as it fought only a few seats and its MPs voted with the Liberals on most issues. During the First World War the Liberal Party split again, a section under Lloyd George staying in government in alliance with the Conservatives, and a section under Asquith going into opposition. In 1918 the Labour Party drove the Asquith Liberals into third place (though neither party did well in the face of an enormous Coalition victory under Lloyd George), and in the era of three-party politics that followed up to 1945 the Liberals never again regained second place. In 1950 they were almost annihilated, surviving only in the Celtic fastnesses of Scotland and Wales. They made a relatively modest comeback in the 1960s and 1970s, culminating in the six million Liberal votes recorded in February 1974.

That is a brief, familiar, and wholly unsatisfactory history of British party politics since 1867. It is unsatisfactory because it concentrates on the politicians and tells us nothing about the voters. To understand British politics we have to know what groups of voters supported which party and why; and we have to be able to trace the decline of old issues and alignments and the rise of new ones. Politicians are talkative people, who naturally have given us very full accounts of what they did and why. But the electorate has no collective means of explaining itself to posterity, and until the first sample surveys thirty years ago there was no systematic way of finding out what voters thought and why they voted in the way they did. But if we do not attempt to find out we are left with only half the picture, and not necessarily the more interesting half.

The politics of the period 1867 to 1918 was to a certain extent class politics; but it was also religious politics, ethnic politics, and rural-urban politics. Each of these factors is worth a short comment, because each has left its mark on present-day voting patterns.

Class conflict. To a large extent, but by no means entirely, the Liberals were the working-class party and the Conservatives the middle-class party. Many of the safest Liberal seats were in mining and heavy industrial areas where working-class voters held a majority even in 1867. In places like Morpeth and Bradford something like the modern class alignment of electoral politics has existed for a century. But many working-class voters supported the Conservatives and their allies, notably in London and Lancashire, and Conservative working-class support rose sharply after the Liberal split of 1886; and even more middle-class voters supported the Liberals, who were historically the party of business and industry. We must look for something other than class to explain these alignments.

Religious conflict. Wars of religion in Britain ended a long time before party politics began, but religious issues still played a role in political argument, and religious divisions were vital at election times. The last important religious quarrel in British politics (if we can disregard Ireland for the moment) was as recently as 1902. In that year nonconformists were involved in massive protests against an Education Act which forced some of them to pay for the upkeep of Anglican schools. As the party of nonconformity in England and Wales, the Liberal Party led the protests. In Scotland divisions in both Church and State followed different lines, but after 1886, broadly speaking, Church of Scotland members supported the Liberal Unionists and Free Church members supported the independent Liberals. The Catholics were mostly also Liberal supporters, though as they were largely Irish this had more to do with ethnic than with religious politics. On the other hand, Anglicans were overwhelmingly Conservative. In Bristol in 1852, three Anglican clergy voted Liberal and fifty-six Conservative; by contrast fourteen Dissenting ministers (and one Catholic priest) had voted Liberal compared to only one Conservative.[1] "The Church of England", as the saying went, "is the Tory Party at prayer". (The sextons, organists and gravediggers of Bristol voted Conservative to a man in 1852.)

[1] Before 1883, the vote was not secret, and enterprising local journalists or booksellers sometimes compiled lists, called pollbooks, showing how every elector had voted. A number of pollbooks, including the one from which these statistics are taken, were collected and published under the title *Pollbooks: how Victorians voted*, ed. J. Vincent, 1967.

Ethnic politics. Wales and Scotland were strongly Liberal, and the Liberals were linked with the movements for Home Rule in both places. But by far the biggest issue was the Irish question (or Question). From the 1870s, the Irish Catholics turned to a party of their own, the Irish Party, to demand Home Rule for Ireland. Ulster Protestants, alarmed that, as they put it, "Home Rule means Rome Rule", were strong Conservatives, and the British Conservative Party supported their position of intransigent opposition to Home Rule. Irish Home Rule was the dominant political issue of the 1880s, culminating in the split of 1886, when the attempt of Gladstone and the Irish Party to pass a Home Rule Bill led to the defection of the Liberal Unionists led by Joseph Chamberlain. The issue remained an explosive one right up to 1914, when Ireland appeared to be on the brink of civil war between Ulster Protestants (supported by the Conservative Party which since 1886 had backed Lord Randolph Churchill's aggressive slogan, "Ulster will fight and Ulster will be right") and the agencies of the Liberal Government which was trying to prepare the way for Home Rule. Only the coming of the First World War, ironically, prevented (or perhaps one should say delayed) an armed conflict in Northern Ireland.

Rural–urban conflict. This lay at the heart of the nineteenth-century struggle between Liberals and Conservatives. The Conservatives were the party of the countryside, the Liberals the party of the towns. The Liberals supported free trade, which meant cheap food (and therefore, from the businessman's point of view, was valuable because it restrained his employees' wage demands). The Conservatives historically favoured Protection, essentially the protection of British agriculture from the effects of cheap grain imports. Again, Liberals wanted a fairer distribution of parliamentary seats, with more going to the burgeoning towns of the industrial north at the expense of the rural south, which was heavily over-represented before 1885. These were questions of conflict between rural and urban interests, and on issues like these middle-class and working-class town-dwellers were on the same side. Free trade and parliamentary reform held master and man together, unlike the class-based issues which would have driven them apart, but the bonds were weakened by the Redistribution Act of 1884 which largely redressed the under-representation of urban areas.

The change from the complex politics just described to the class politics of today was a long and slow one, and it is not yet complete – and for this reason one must know something about nineteenth-century voting patterns in order to understand modern British elections. From 1886 onwards the class division gradually became more and more important at the expense of all the others. As the working classes got the vote, their leaders brought forward a new range of demands which it was difficult to accommodate within the old political structure: statutory restrictions on the hours of the working day, or protection of the legal status of trade unions, to give two examples. At first, working-class politicians operated through the Liberal Party, a fact which no doubt helped to drive businessmen and industrialists into the arms of the Liberal Unionists or the Conservatives. By 1906 the Liberals were to a large extent a working-class party; they depended on working-class votes and they put forward social reform measures in the interests of the working-class. But eventually they succumbed to the Labour Party, which could do all these things but also had a genuine working-class leadership, which the Liberals never achieved. By 1918 the lines of modern class politics had been drawn, with the Conservatives as the middle-class and Labour as the working-class party.

Other alignments

Nevertheless, traces of the old alignments remain. As was said earlier, most electors are powerfully influenced by the political environment in which they are brought up. What, then, has happened to voters who were brought up in the days of Liberal and Conservative politics? If they are active nonconformists, there is a strong chance that they will still be Liberal supporters. Generally speaking, Liberal support is drawn very evenly from all age groups and all social classes, but there is a residue of Liberal strength among elderly nonconformists. This is one survival of the old religious politics. Catholic voters are also distinctive; they are amongst the most strongly pro-Labour of any group. Of course, many Catholics are working-class, and would be expected to be Labour supporters in any case; but in fact their support of Labour goes beyond what might be guessed from their class position. Whatever their social class, Catholics are more pro-Labour than non-Catholics. On the other hand the link between Anglicanism and Conservative voting also persists, at least for the minority of Anglicans whose adherence is any more than nominal. If a Church of England member goes to church at all, he (or more often she) is fairly likely to be a Conservative supporter; and the more faithful a churchgoer, the more likely the elector is to vote Conservative.

Old regional alignments have not only survived, but have re-emerged in an accentuated form. The recent rise of Scottish and Welsh nationalism is perhaps best regarded as a modern phenomenon, and is dealt with later in this chapter. There is nothing modern, however, about the political alignments which have emerged since 1968 in Northern Ireland – indeed, they reek very strongly of the seventeenth century. As was noted in chapter 2, class is hardly an issue at all in Northern Ireland politics. The dominant issue is religion, and this is crosscut by the question of willingness to abide by constitutional procedures. The Protestants, who comprise about two-thirds of the Northern Ireland electorate, have, since the crisis of 1886, given their support solidly to the Unionist party. But within that party, sometimes on the surface, sometimes concealed, there has always been a conflict between those prepared to go beyond normal constitutional means to get their way and those unwilling to do so. It is the first group who are now regarded as "Loyalists", though their loyalty can take paradoxical forms. In 1914, for instance, Ulster Protestants demonstrated their loyalty to the British Crown by shipping large quantities of arms from Germany to Northern Ireland, under the noses of the British authorities, in order to put up armed resistance to the British Government's Home Rule Bill, which was finally enacted in September 1914. In the long period of unchallenged Unionist rule over the Northern Ireland Parliament from 1920 to 1969, the divergences between "constitutionalist" and "paramilitary" Unionists did not come to the surface because nobody was seriously interfering with what the Unionists wanted to do. But from the outbreak in 1968 of the current crisis, successive British governments have always been urging the Ulster Unionists to take steps, such as disarming the special constabulary or sharing power with the Catholic community, which they have been unwilling to take. So the division has deepened between those who are prepared, in the last resort, to comply with the British government's requests, and those who were described as "Loyalists", yet are prepared to defy the British regime. As we saw in chapter 2, the elections to the Northern

Ireland Assembly of 1973, held under the newly introduced single transferable vote system, encouraged an open and final breach between these factions.

Within the Catholic third of the Northern Ireland electorate a similar split has always existed. Catholics were hostile to the setting up of the state of Northern Ireland in 1920; naturally, they had been looking forward to the Home Rule which had been promised for the whole of Ireland, in which they would have been part of a large majority rather than a small and often persecuted minority. Some Catholic politicians argued that they should take part in Northern Ireland politics and get what they could out of the system on their constituents' behalf – as does the Social Democratic and Labour Party today. But others thought that Catholics should have nothing to do with the institutions of the Stormont regime, should refuse to take their seats if elected, and should work for the overthrow of the state, by force if necessary, the position today of both the "Official" and the "Provisional" wings of Sinn Fein, and of their respective branches of the IRA. It should be noted that, whereas in the Protestant community the "Loyalists" now heavily outnumber the constitutionalists, among Catholic voters the SDLP has far greater support than any of the factions of the IRA when voters are forced to make a direct choice between them.

Northern Ireland, then, is an obvious exception to the pattern of class politics in Britain. But in recent years, observers have been wondering whether the general pattern has been breaking down in other ways also. The first version of the argument was the so-called *embourgeoisement* hypothesis. After the Labour Party had lost three elections in a row – in 1951, 1955, and 1959 – some observers thought that greater prosperity among working-class voters was leading them to desert the Labour Party, with its class-based appeal rooted in the poverty and deprivation of the prewar years. The Conservatives, with their campaign slogan, "Life's Better with the Conservatives – Don't Let Labour Ruin It" were thought to have hit a winning streak. As workers became more affluent, owning cars and refrigerators, so they became more *bourgeois*, and more likely to support the Conservatives.

The *embourgeoisement* argument was dented by the fact that Labour won the elections of 1964 and 1966, although the workers had become more affluent still by that time. Subsequent writers drew a distinction between the affluent worker at home and at work. A worker may acquire the trappings of a more prosperous way of life at home; but at work he is still the underdog, still a person with no responsibility for the work he does, who has to take orders from a foreman. In these circumstances he is still likely to retain his feeling of class solidarity and his propensity to vote Labour. "Class identification", as Pulzer has aptly said, "is too firmly rooted to be overturned by the arrival of a washing machine". While this is certainly true, the loyalty of voters of all classes to "their" party has clearly become more conditional. Voters are less likely to cast their votes as an act of faith and more likely to scrutinise the claims of politicians and the extent to which they are fulfilled in reality. In this sense, the electorate as a whole is becoming more "secular" in its attitudes, to use the term mentioned earlier in this chapter. Whether working-class or middle-class, Labour or Conservative, voters are becoming more sceptical and less likely automatically to endorse the party of their class than they were twenty years ago. Class politics has actually declined from its peak at the general elections of 1950 and 1951. Today fewer people vote at all (turnout dropped steadily at every election till 1970, and in February 1974 rose again, but only to the level it attained in 1959), and the fluctuations of party support and popularity are much greater than they were in the 1950s.

One way of explaining these changes is to say that some voters are moving from an acquisitive to a post-bourgeois attitude to politics. The idea behind this piece of jargon is roughly this: older voters who remember the last war and the poverty and unemployment of the prewar years are primarily interested in security and prosperity – a set of views labelled an "acquisitive" orientation – whereas younger voters who have not lived through the 1930s or the Second World War are less interested in economic objectives of this sort. Their politics, called "post-bourgeois", may embrace a wide range of objectives: free speech, less pollution, independence for small nations, more permissive legislation on drugs or sex, for instance. Such voters will be much less tied to traditional class parties, especially parties of the right such as the Conservatives.

This looks an attractive explanation for the Liberal and Nationalist upsurge of 1974: in February 1974, as readers will recall, minor parties got 7·5 million votes and thirty-seven seats. More voters than ever before rejected the class-based parties. The Conservatives, with

38 per cent of the vote, had their worst performance since 1929; and the Labour Party, which won the election of February 1974, nevertheless did so with only 37 per cent of the votes cast, which was *its* lowest share of the vote since its catastrophic defeat in 1931, and considerably less than in its years of defeat such as 1959 and 1970. In the Liberal and Nationalist successes of 1974 we may see a fusion of a very old tradition in British politics with a very new one: the minor-party vote is partly a "pre-class" one and partly a "post-class" one.

All three of the newly successful parties owed something to old traditions. The Liberal tradition has survived unbroken from the nineteenth century in some rural areas, notably in Wales, where voting Liberal is linked with strong support of nonconformist chapels and Welsh culture, and Lloyd George is still remembered as the greatest politician of the century. The Scottish National Party was founded in 1928, in the wake of many years of sporadic Liberal agitation for Scottish home rule. The Welsh nationalist party Plaid Cymru ("Party of Wales") dates from the same period, and has even stronger links with nineteenth-century ethnic and religious politics. Plaid Cymru is in a way a very old-fashioned party. Its real base is in rural north and west Wales, whose inhabitants speak Welsh, attend chapel, and keep the pubs closed on Sundays. Caernarvon, Merioneth, and Carmarthen, the seats Plaid Cymru holds or has held, are places which twentieth-century political controversies have barely touched – not that they are any the worse for that. In urban Wales and in the mining valleys, where some of the most acute class conflicts in Britain have arisen in the past, Plaid Cymru has made much less progress.

But, aside from these links with nineteenth-century politics, all three minor parties have made great strides in recent elections, reflecting the decline in class voting. Young voters have been particularly attracted to the Liberal and Nationalist parties. One survey of people voting for the first time in 1974 found that 20 per cent of them voted Liberal and 5 per cent Nationalist,[1] compared with 20 per cent

[1] That is, 5 per cent in Great Britain as a whole. But Scotland and Wales between them have only one-sixth of the British electorate. Assuming no respondent in England was proposing to vote nationalist, therefore, the level of nationalist support among young voters in Scotland and Wales was presumably as high as 30 per cent.

Conservative and 36 per cent Labour. The youngest voters are more likely to support Liberals and Nationalists than any other age group. Also, the rise in the Liberal vote was greater among the best-educated voters than among those who had left school at earlier ages. These statistics give some support to the notion of "post-bourgeois" voting: that is, that young well-educated people who have never experienced war or poverty are breaking away from the old class alignments and supporting parties whose promise is not economic security, but something much more exciting – national self-determination, for example.

But we must not be carried away by novel theories. If post-bourgeois voting had accounted for a lot of the Scottish Nationalist vote, it would not have slumped so heavily in 1979. There are reasons much more mundane than post-bourgeois voting to explain much of the minor parties' support. A lot of it was undoubtedly the product of frustration with both main parties, and with their inability to do anything about inflation. The Scottish Nationalists benefited enormously from the discovery of North Sea oil – "It's Scotland Oil", as their slogan insisted – which gave them the powerful argument that if Scotland became independent, it could use oil income to get out of the economic problems besetting the United Kingdom at present. Most voting in 1974 was conditioned not by affluence but by austerity, and this is unlikely to change in the near future.

The concept of political generations

In chapter 5 we shall look in more detail at the short-term problems, including the state of the economy, which exercise a big influence on voting. But first let us look more carefully at a point which has been touched on more than once in the present chapter. In discussing the working-class Conservative vote, we pointed to the number of elderly working-class people who vote Conservative, and suggested that this arose not because they had changed their views but because they had *not* changed their views. In other words, they had come to maturity in a world in which the party struggle was between Conservatives and Liberals, with the Labour Party a small organisation which fought only a few constituencies. (Out of over 600 seats, Labour fought only fifteen in 1900, fifty-one in 1906, and seventy-eight and fifty-six in the two elections of 1910. Not until 1918 did the majority of voters have a Labour candidate to pick if they wished to.) This is a fundamental point, which is often missed. Most people inherit their political views from their families. Students often find this difficult to believe. Often they themselves are in revolt from everything their parents stand for, from hairstyles to political opinions; but the fact remains that such people are in a small minority. If I am asked to guess how you vote, and am allowed to learn one, but only one fact about you, the best thing for me to ask is "How did your father vote?" The answer to that question gives me a better chance than any other of predicting correctly how you will vote. Most people form political opinions in their adolescent years, and therefore we must look at the political worlds in which various generations of today's voters grew up.

A voter born in 1900 came to adulthood in a world of Conservative –Liberal competition, with the Labour Party existing only as a small third party. The chances of his being brought up in a Labour-voting household would be very slim. Such people comprised a large part of the electorate ten years ago, but their numbers are being rapidly reduced by death. This means that the Labour Party is improving its position relative to the Conservatives, irrespective of the way in which voters are changing their minds. As we shall see in chapter 5, it is quite possible for there to be a "swing to Labour" during which more voters switch from Labour to Conservative than *vice versa*. This is because of the dying-off of a predominantly Conservative generation and its replacement by a generation with a substantial Labour majority.

A voter born in 1910 would have spent his formative years during the period of three-party politics in which the Liberals were slowly losing the struggle to remain as the principal opposition to the Conservatives. Like older voters, he may have been brought up in a Liberal household, and at some time have had to make the choice between Labour and the Conservatives. As far as we can tell, rather more traditional Liberal supporters opted for the Conservatives than for Labour when forced to make the choice. Voters born around 1910, then, are more likely than older, but less likely than younger men and women to have spent their adolescence in a Labour environment.

Voters born in the 1920s had their lives moulded by the politics of the Second World War. Like the First, that war had a profound effect on the British party system. Between 1940 and 1944 there occurred a decisive leftward shift in the voting behaviour of the British electorate. Perhaps the war effort created its own kind of welfare state, coupled to a new sense of fraternity, and also showed that strict planning of the economy could work. The shift to the left was not immediately obvious, because officially there was a party truce, and the parties were not fighting each other at by-elections. But it became plain in 1945 when the Labour Party won its first-ever clear election victory with a huge majority of seats and a substantial (by British standards) majority of votes. Voters born in the late 1920s form the most pro-Labour political generation of all.

Younger voters entered the electorate under a party system in which Labour and the Conservatives were fighting on more or less equal terms. Their chances of being brought up in anything other than a Labour- or Conservative-voting household were very slight. But since Labour has never regained the peak level of support it touched in 1945, the generations of voters born in 1940 and later are not quite so strongly pro-Labour as their immediate elders. And, as we saw earlier in this chapter, the youngest voters of all have the most diverse range of political views of any generation in the electorate.

The concept of political generations which we have been exploring is very valuable for the way it teaches us to look at familiar statistics about age, class and party in a new light. We can see that British voting behaviour is very complex, and historically conditioned in complicated and unexpected ways. Today's electorate simultaneously contains pensioners whose voting is rooted in the Liberal–Conservative fights of the last century, middle-aged voters who most firmly belong to the era of class politics, and young people whose voting may even belong to a post-class political generation. But there is yet more to be learnt from the study of political generations, because we must also study the lessons of demography – that is, the study of life expectancy, birth and death rates, fertility and so on. These affect voters in different ways, an obvious fact which has a perhaps unsuspected relevance to elections.

Let us take life expectancy first. On average, women live longer than men; also on average, the higher the social class into which a baby is born, the longer he can be expected to live. Both these factors have political implications; both favour the Conservatives. In Britain, as in every other democracy for which statistics exist, women are more likely to favour the party of the right than men. In 1970, for instance, 47·3 per cent of male voters supported Labour and 42·2 per cent voted Conservative; the figures for women were 40·6 per cent and 40·9 per cent respectively. Obviously, too, people of high social class are more likely than any others to support the Conservatives. In fact, it has been estimated that the average Conservative voter lives long enough to vote in thirteen general elections, whereas the average Labour voter only survives for twelve.

But life expectancy is balanced by fertility. On average, working-class parents have more children than middle-class ones, a fact which benefits Labour. Not only that, but within the working class it has been found that Labour voters tend to have more children than Conservatives. So, while differences in life expectancy favour the Conservatives, differences in the birth rate favour Labour.

The other factors which change the composition of the electorate (disregarding imprisonment or succession to the peerage, both of which disqualify their victims from voting) are emigration and immigration. So far as we can tell, emigration has little effect on the balance of party support; but immigration is another matter. Up to twenty-five years ago, the largest category of immigrants in Britain was Irish. Irishmen in Britain tend to be strong Labour supporters, both because they are mostly working-class and for historical reasons: Labour is the natural heir of the Liberal Party, which the Irish in Britain were always encouraged to support in the nineteenth century because it was the party of Home Rule, as against the Conservatives, who supported the Orangemen of Protestant Ulster. The political position of Asian and West Indian Commonwealth immigrants is more complex. When they first arrived in Britain, their impact on voting was small; many of them were not listed on the electoral register at all, and of those who were very few voted. Nowadays, turnout among Commonwealth immigrants (especially West Indians) is higher, and strongly pro-Labour; but there has also been an anti-immigrant backlash which clearly cost Labour one or two seats (the best-known example being Smethwick in 1964, won against the general trend by an all-but-openly racialist Conservative candidate) and which may, overall, have lost one or two per cent of Labour's supporters to the Conservatives.

Thus the demographic forces affecting voting behaviour are

complex and work in several conflicting directions at once. As we shall see in chapter 5, they are among the numerous factors which go to make up that elusive concept, the swing of the pendulum from one election to the next.

5 Swings and Roundabouts: short-term shifts in voting behaviour

How to measure electoral change

We commonly talk of an election as if it were a single event. "The election of 1945 showed that . . ." and so on. Yet it is not really a single event at all. Every general election involves 635 constituency contests; every constituency contest involves at least around 20,000 votes and often many more. The measure most commonly used to summarise the effect of the millions of decisions which go to make up a general election result is "swing", which is used to show how uniform change is across the country. In most general elections since the war political change has been impressively uniform from one constituency to the next. If Ebbw Vale has registered a 4 per cent swing from Labour to the Conservatives, so has Eastbourne. This political uniformity is relatively new; it only became impressive in the 1930s, and the elections of 1974 and 1979 mark the beginning of a return to wider regional and individual variations. The Davies, Taverne and Milne cases mentioned in chapter 2 may also herald a new lease of life for the independent MP, but in general the electorate still votes for the party, not the man, and it is rare for an unusually good (or bad) MP to have much impact on the uniform swing.

Yet appearances may be deceptive. Behind small, uniform swings in the country as a whole there lurk complicated currents and cross-currents which may between them include as much as 30 or 40 per cent of the electorate. To see why this is so, we must first understand how swing is calculated.

There are in fact several ways of doing it, but the commonest is that used by the TV networks on general election nights, which will be familiar to those who follow these all-night endurance tests. To calculate swing, we add together one major party's gain in votes since the last election and the other major party's loss, and divide the result by 2. (All the calculations are in percentages.) If the general trend were (say) to Labour, then swing would be the average

Table 5.1. *The calculation of swing*

A. *Straight fight*

	Election 1 %	Election 2 %
Cons	51	49
Lab	49	51
Lib	—	—
	100	100

Swing to Labour: $\dfrac{(51-49)+(51-49)}{2}$

$=2\%$

B. *Third party intervenes*

	Election 1 %	Election 2 %
Cons	55	40
Lab	45	35
Lib	—	25
	100	100

Swing to Labour: $\dfrac{(55-40)+(35-45)}{2}$

$=2\cdot5\%$

C. *Third party withdraws*

	Election 1 %	Election 2 %
Cons	45	55
Lab	30	45
Lib	25	—
	100	100

Swing to Labour: $\dfrac{(45-55)+(45-30)}{2}$

$=2\cdot5\%$

of the Labour gain and the Conservative loss in shares of the total vote. In this case, any stray pro-Conservative swings would be denoted by minus signs. The whole idea is more clearly expressed in figures. Examples of the calculation of swing are shown in Table 5.1.

Swing, then, measures the change in the relative position of the leading parties in every variety of contest. If there is a straight fight both times, one party's loss is of course exactly the same as the other party's gain, in terms of share of the votes cast. If a third party intervenes or withdraws, the position is more complicated. In Example B, for instance, the votes of *both* main parties declined and in Example C they both rose. But the Conservative share declined more, or rose less, than the Labour share, and the result is a net swing to Labour on both occasions.

The concept of swing has been fiercely attacked. Many of the attacks are beside the point because, although it is true that swing cannot aspire to measure *every* variety of change that goes on, it does enable us to compare the results in Abertillery, Argyllshire, and Ashby-de-la-Zouch. No other measure yet devised can do this. Nevertheless, the concept *can* be misleading if people read into it things that are not there. The commonest mistake is to assume that all change results from direct switching – that in Example A, for instance, the change was caused by 2 per cent of the voters ceasing to support the Conservatives and voting Labour instead. The truth is far more complex. We have mentioned a number of movements which give rise to swing. People die and others come of age. If more Conservative than Labour voters die, and more Labour voters than Conservatives come on to the electoral register, these two movements create a swing to Labour just as surely as direct switching. Likewise every former Conservative who now votes Liberal or abstains represents a gain for Labour, and every former Labour voter who does one of these things represents a gain for the Conservatives. The best way to understand how diverse are the possible sources of electoral change is to construct a table, called a "matrix", which provides a complete picture of change from one election to the next. The matrix includes everyone who was in the electorate at some time between Election 1 and Election 2, both inclusive. The descriptions on the lefthand side of the table relate to how people voted at Election 1, and are all self-explanatory except "Too young". This

Table 5.2. *A matrix of electoral change*

Election 1	Election 2					
	Cons	Lab	Lib	Other	Abstain	Dead
Cons	1					
Lab		2				
Lib			3			
Other				4		
Abstain					5	
Too Young						6

1. Constant Conservative
2. Constant Labour
3. Constant Liberal
4. Constant other party
5. Constant abstainer
6. Never available to vote

denotes people who are not yet in the electorate at Election 1 but who later enter it in time to vote at Election 2. Reading the matrix from left to right will tell us about each of these categories: for instance, a Conservative voter at Election 1 must either vote Conservative, Liberal, Labour or for another party at Election 2; or he may abstain; or he may be dead, and hence not available to vote. The numbers of people in each category, represented as percentages of the entire combined electorate covered by the matrix, would be found in the six cells along the top row of the matrix. Between them, the categories cover every possible thing that could happen to an elector who voted Conservative at Election 1.[1]

The table can also be read from top to bottom. At the head of each column is a description of the different ways people can behave at Election 2. The first column, for instance, represents all those who vote Conservative at Election 2. Reading down the column, we see that at Election 1 they may have been Conservative, Labour, Liberal

[1] "Too young" also covers other means of entering the electorate, such as immigration and naturalisation; and "Dead" covers other means of leaving it, such as imprisonment and succession to the peerage. A faulty electoral register could also keep potential voters out of the electorate at one time or another. For instance, many Asian Commonwealth immigrants have been erroneously omitted from electoral registers in the past.

or other-party supporters; they may have abstained; or they may have been too young to vote.

In Table 5.2 there are thirty-six cells. This means that there are thirty-six possible combinations of behaviour (if dying can be counted as a form of behaviour) at the two elections; but only six of these involve no change. These will be found on the diagonal line – known as the "principal diagonal" – running from top left to bottom right on the diagram. (In practice, though, if any unfortunate citizen occupies the bottom righthand cell – too young to vote at Election 1 and dead at Election 2 – he is unlikely to be discovered by people conducting surveys. This cell will thus be given a value of zero in the actual matrices we shall illustrate.) Apart from the six on the principal diagonal, all the cells contain people whose voting behaviour changes, and who therefore make a contribution to the fluctuation in party fortunes.

If we could construct a matrix of electoral change between every pair of elections, we could discard the concept of swing altogether, because we would have a much more accurate and comprehensive measure. Unfortunately we cannot. The only way to find out how many voters fall into each cell is to conduct a sample survey and ask them – that is, contact exactly the same set of electors at two successive elections and find out what proportion have changed their vote. But this is an elaborate and expensive operation, and is rarely possible. However, we do have the results of one series of surveys of

Table 5.3. *Electoral change, 1966–70*

	1970 election				
1966 election	Cons	Lab	Lib	Other or Abstained	Dead, etc.
Cons	19·1	0·8	0·4	3·7	2·8
Lab	3·2	18·0	0·8	6·5	2·9
Lib	1·5	0·7	2·0	1·1	0·3
Other or Abstained	3·5	3·5	1·1	12·1	1·0
Too Young etc.	3·5	5·9	0·8	4·8	0·0

100·0

Source: Adapted from Butler & Stokes, *Political Change in Britain*, 2nd edn, Macmillan, 1974, p. 263.

this sort, which were carried out by Butler and Stokes between 1959 and 1970 for their important book *Political Change in Britain*. The results give us by far the fullest and most valuable picture of electoral change we possess. An example of Butler and Stokes's findings is given in Table 5.3. Readers may at first sight find the matrix notation baffling; they ought to persevere. It is not hard to understand, and the results are extremely valuable.

Labour won the general election of 1966 by ninety seats with 6 per cent more votes than the Conservatives; the next election in 1970 was narrowly won by the Conservatives who beat Labour by forty-three seats, which represented a 3·5 per cent lead in votes. Table 5·3 shows in detail how this came about.[1]

Direct switching. 3·2 per cent of the electorate (row 2, column 1)[2] switched from Labour to Conservative, but 0·8 per cent (row 1, column 2) switched from Conservative to Labour. Thus the net switch was 2·4 per cent, so that the change in the Labour lead was —4·8 per cent. Every Labour loss was also a Conservative gain, so these voters have to be counted twice.

Circulation of Liberals. The Conservatives gained 1·5 per cent (p_{31}) (see note 2 below for an explanation of this notation) minus 0·4 per cent (p_{13}). Labour gained 0·7 per cent (p_{32}) minus 0·8 per cent (p_{23}). Net outcome: —1·2 per cent in Labour lead.

Abstainers. The Conservatives gained 3·5 per cent (p_{41}) minus 3·7 per cent (p_{14}). Labour gained 3·5 per cent (p_{42}) minus 6·5 per cent (p_{24}). Net outcome: —2·8 per cent in Labour lead.

Changes in electorate. This element reflects the demographic changes described at length in chapter 4. The Conservatives gained 3·5 per

---

[1] Lynx-eyed readers may have noticed that the percentage differences between the parties in Table 5.3 are not the same as the actual percentages quoted in this paragraph. Without being too technical, the reasons are: (*a*) the matrices are derived from a sample survey, which is liable to sampling error (see pp. 73–74 below); (*b*) the figures in the matrix are percentages of the combined electorate (including abstainers etc) at both elections; but the actual percentage leads were percentages of those voting at each election.

[2] The cells are conventionally described as p_{12}, p_{21} etc. In this notation p denotes a cell, the first number denotes the row of the entry, and the second number denotes the column. Thus p_{21} is the entry to be found in the first column of the second row, which is 3·2.

cent (p_{51}) from new voters and lost 2·8 per cent (p_{15}) through deaths. But Labour did much better. It gained 5·9 per cent (p_{52}) from new voters and lost 2·9 per cent (p_{25}) through deaths. The net outcome was a *gain* of 2·3 per cent in the Labour lead.

Putting all these factors together, we get the following picture:

	Net change in Labour lead, %
Direct switching	—4·8
Circulation of Liberals	—1·2
Circulation of abstainers	—2·8
Changes in electorate	+2·3
Net change in Labour lead	—6·5

This drop of 6·5 per cent was enough to turn a comfortable Labour victory in 1966 into a narrow Conservative one in 1970. In this case direct switching and abstention by former Labour supporters were the biggest causes of the swing, but they were partly offset by demographic factors. This is what we should expect from the analysis of long-term change in chapter 4. The Labour Party stands to benefit from such things as the dying off of the last generations to come to maturity before Labour was a national party, and the higher birth rate among Labour than Conservative supporters.

As a matter of fact, the 1970 election represented a considerable recovery for the Labour Party. In 1968 and 1969 it had had the worst electoral record of any modern government, losing by-elections by large majorities and plunging to unprecedented depths in the opinion polls. Butler and Stokes conducted a survey in 1969, between the 1966 and 1970 results we have just examined. Naturally, this showed a heavy swing against Labour. By far the biggest element in this swing involved abstention. Droves of voters who had supported Labour told the investigators in 1969 that they intended to abstain. But by 1970 this gap had almost been made up. The abstainers of 1969 were by this time returning to Labour in almost as large numbers as they had earlier flocked away. Therefore these two changes virtually cancelled each other out, and consequently make no impact on the statistics just quoted. Indeed, the longer the period over which we measure electoral change, the more these short-term changes do cancel each other out, so that the direction of the long-term trends becomes clear. We can see this if we look at one more matrix, this time showing the pathways of change over the whole period from 1959 (when the Conservatives had a majority of about 100) to 1970 (when they had a lead of forty-three over Labour, and thirty over all their opponents put together).

Table 5.4. *Electoral change, 1959–70*

	1970 election				
1959 election	*Cons*	*Lab*	*Lib*	*Other or Abstained*	*Dead etc.*
Cons	14·9	1·4	1·3	4·4	7·1
Lab	2·0	11·6	0·6	6·3	6·2
Lib	0·7	0·6	0·7	0·8	0·8
Other or Abstained	3·3	2·8	0·5	7·7	1·9
Too Young etc.	6·9	9·7	1·5	6·3	0·0

100·0

Source: Adapted from Butler & Stokes, *op. cit.*

We shall not repeat the previous line-by-line analysis; the interested reader should be able to do so for himself. In summary, however, the changes from 1959 to 1970 were as follows:

	Net change in Labour lead, %
Direct switching	−1·2
Circulation of Liberals	+0·6
Circulation of abstainers	−2·4
Changes in electorate	+3·7
Net change in Labour lead	+0·7

What do these figures mean? They show that the Conservatives gained from direct switching and from movements involving abstentions (for instance, Labour lost 6·3 per cent of the electorate to abstention but the Conservatives lost only 4·4 per cent). But the overall 'Conservative lead was diminished, not increased. This was because changes in the composition of the electorate benefited Labour substantially. Among new voters, 9·7 per cent supported Labour and only 6·9 per cent the Conservatives; among voters who died during the period, 7·1 per cent had been Conservative supporters and only 6·2 per cent Labour. This confirms our argument about long-term factors which have benefited the Labour Party. Nineteen fifty-nine was a bad year for Labour; one might have expected it to gain converts from among the existing electorate, but it did not; it was actually losing its appeal to those who were already in the electorate and stayed in it for the next eleven years. If the electorate of 1959 had voted in the 1970 election, the Conservatives would have triumphed by a margin of 150 seats or more. Only the constant change and renewal of the electorate saved the Labour Party by holding the actual Conservative majority down to forty-three over Labour. The Butler and Stokes surveys contain striking and neglected evidence for a long-term erosion of the Labour vote, which the 1974 and 1979 elections seem to confirm.

Measures of short-term change: by-elections
The statistics we have been examining show what a complex mixture of long-term and short-term changes goes to make up every election result. We have already looked at long-term change; it remains to say something about short-term fluctuations.

A general election is usually held only every four or five years, although in 1966 and October 1974 elections were called at much shorter intervals because the preceding election had not given any party a clear majority. However, there are plenty of indications in between elections of the standing of the parties. The three principal measures are by-elections, local elections and opinion polls. A word should be said about the usefulness of each of these as a measure of public opinion about the parties.

By-elections are most commonly held when MPs die in office or resign. The number of by-elections held is smaller than it used to be. This is partly because some causes of by-elections (such as MPs succeeding to the peerage) are now rare, but more because Governments have suffered such stunning losses in by-elections in the last ten years that they try to avoid having them whenever they can. At present there are usually about eight or ten by-elections a year.

The biggest difference between by-elections and general elections is that the former do not directly decide which party will form the government (although the Labour government of October 1974 had lost its majority by 1977 because of by-election losses. It was not defeated on a confidence motion until March 1979, but its last two years of life depended on pacts and deals with other parties). Voters do not treat by-elections in the same way as general elections. Usually, though not always, the turnout at by-elections is lower than at general elections in the same constituency, and the major parties, especially the party in power, often do badly because their supporters stay at home. But by-elections are often excellent for parties such as the Liberals and Nationalists. The most spectacular by-elections in recent years have been those in which Liberals and Nationalists have captured formerly safe seats from the major parties. For example, Gwynfor Evans won Carmarthen for Plaid Cymru in 1966; Winifred Ewing won Hamilton as a Scottish Nationalist in 1967; and the Liberals have triumphed in a number of by-elections such as Isle of Ely and Berwick-on-Tweed in 1973 and Liverpool Edge Hill in 1979. Often, indeed, minor parties do better at by-elections than at the following general election, and their best results frequently occur in what were previously safe seats. This may sound paradoxical, but is easy to understand. For an example of how the safeness of the seat affected voters' calculations, we may look at the Berwick-on-Tweed division, a safe Conservative seat where a by-election took place in 1973 because of the resignation of Mr Anthony Lambton (known to his friends as Lord Lambton) after he had admitted to accusations of associating with prostitutes and possessing cannabis. (It is not, of course, a legal offence for an MP to have intercourse with a prostitute; but, since he was a junior defence minister, Lambton risked being blackmailed or having defence secrets passed on to hostile powers.) At the by-election, it is plain that a large number of Conservative voters supported the Liberal, many of them no doubt feeling that as it was a safe seat it could do the party no harm for them to register their protest in this way. But at the same time Labour voters could see that their party had no chance of winning and that it was in their best interests to vote Liberal "to keep the Tories out". With both these processes working it was probably easier for the Liberal to win the seat than if it had been marginal as between Conservative and Labour. In these circumstances, by-election results may even exaggerate the unpopularity of the two main parties.

Measure of short-term change: local elections

The second frequently cited barometer of public opinion is the annual cycle of local election results. Since local government was reorganised in 1973 (1974 in Scotland), all councillors serve for a term of four years. In some places, all councillors retire together every four years; in others, there is a cycle of elections involving county and district councillors every year. Every May, therefore, there are local elections in one or another part of the country. In many places, especially in rural areas, local elections are not fought on party political lines. Many local councillors (although probably a diminishing number) still think it is wrong that party politics should intrude on local elections. But this attitude is not really practicable in large towns and cities, where individual wards must be too big for candidates to be able to know their electors on a personal, non-political basis. In most towns, local elections have been fought on a conventional party political basis for many years now (although in some places, including Bristol, South Shields and the Scottish cities, the role of the Conservatives has been filled by local right-wing parties with various names).

Although it is often mortifying for local politicians to have to admit it, local election results are usually closely related to the performance of the government of the day, and hardly at all related to the performance of the party in office at the town hall. When, for instance, Labour is in government and doing badly, then good, bad and indifferent Labour-controlled local authorities are all equally vulnerable to a uniform swing to the Conservatives. Thus the local election results are closely scrutinised, in the same way as by-elections, for the trends they reveal. One word of warning about these trends: local election turnout is usually low, often around 40 per cent. A large proportion of the swing in these elections is due to differential abstention – that is, to supporters of the more unpopular party (usually the party forming the government of the day) simply staying at home.

The general pattern in local election swing is always the same. The government of the day does badly in mid-term, and recovers in the run-up to the next general election. This has a clear impact on the pattern of local politics in Britain: they tend to mirror national politics, with a time-lag of two or three years. This is because of the relationship between councillors' terms of office and the national popularity of the parties at the time when they come up for election. Thus in 1963 Labour did well in local elections because of the unpopularity of the then Tory government. A slide in Labour popularity in 1965 and 1966 started, reaching an all-time low in 1968 when hardly a single Labour councillor succeeded in getting re-elected in cities like Birmingham and Bradford. With the Conservative victory in the 1970 general election, Labour started doing well again in local elections; 1971 and 1972 were very good years for the Labour Party, and 1973, when the first elections were held for the new English and Welsh counties and districts which took power in 1974, was only slightly less good.

The cycle was repeated under the 1974–79 Labour governments, when the Conservatives swept the country in the 1976 to 1978 local elections. But since councillors serve for a four-year term, this cycle contains an inbuilt time-lag. For instance, the Conservative councillors elected in the anti-Labour landslide of 1968 did not face re-election till 1971 (the term of office used to be three years instead of the present four). So the Conservatives kept control of many towns and cities long after the pendulum had swung to Labour. Local elections play a double role in British politics. They give a useful impression of the popularity of the government, but they also decide which party rules in Britain's town and county halls – in a way which is largely a reflection of public opinion about the national government.

The uses and abuses of opinion polls

The most familiar measure of public opinion is also the most controversial: the opinion poll. Several polls, of which the best-known are Gallup and NOP (National Opinion Polls) make regular surveys of public opinion. They ask, "If there were a general election tomorrow, how would you vote?", and this is often coupled with questions about the popularity of the party leaders; the results are published regularly in several newspapers. They show even wider fluctuations in party support than do by-elections and local elections. For instance, after the famous Orpington by-election of 1962 when the Liberals snatched a safe Conservative seat, the polls actually put the Liberals ahead of both the other parties. And in the depth of the Labour trough of 1968, the polls showed the Conservatives as being 23 per cent ahead of Labour. If that result had been confirmed by a general election, the Conservatives would have had an overwhelming majority of over 300 seats.

Many students are deeply suspicious of opinion poll findings. (So, indeed, are many politicians, especially when the polls claim that public opinion differs from the politicians' estimates of it.) Let us look at the two criticisms which are most frequently made of opinion polls.

1. "Nobody has ever approached *me* in an opinion poll. How am I to know that the results they get are a fair sample of what the population as a whole thinks?" When opinion polling first started people thought they would have to contact a vast number of voters in order to get a fair idea of the views of the electorate as a whole. This idea was shattered by the notorious *Literary Digest* poll of 1936. The *Literary Digest*, an American magazine, contacted over two million Americans by telephone to ask how they intended to vote in the presidential election of that year. Their result predicted an easy win for the Republicans; but in fact F. D. Roosevelt scored a sweeping Democratic victory. Contacting two million people had proved neither necessary nor sufficient for an accurate prediction. The *Literary Digest* went wrong because it failed to ensure that the people it approached were representative of the whole population. Everybody it telephoned, needless to say, possessed a telephone. But telephones, in 1936, were mostly owned by the rich, and the rich mostly voted Republican. But the poor, who had no telephones, strongly favoured the Democrats.

At the same time other pollsters, sampling only about 2,000 voters, had correctly predicted that the Democrats would win. They, like all modern opinion pollsters, had taken great care to make sure that their sample was representative: that the proportion of women, old people, working-class voters, and so on was the same in the sample as in the population as a whole. If you have got a fair sample you can make a reliable prediction. Nowadays there are two main ways of getting a fair sample. One is to send interviewers out with strict instructions as to the sorts of people they must interview. If 60 per cent of the electorate is working-class, say, then 60 per cent of those the interviewer selects must also be working-class. This is called "quota sampling". The other way, called "random" or "probability" sampling, is to take the electoral register as a basis, draw names from it in a strictly controlled way (electoral number 23 and every 37th number thereafter, for instance) and send interviewers to the people selected in this way and to them alone. In this way again a fair sample can be obtained.

Readers may still be sceptical. If 2,000 voters are drawn at random from the electoral register, there is no logical reason why they should not all be Tories. What guarantee can there be that a random sample will not be unlucky in this way? The answer lies in a statistical theory which states that if a very large number of different probability samples is drawn from the same population, the great majority of them will closely reflect the distribution of whatever characteristic is being examined in the population as a whole. For example 95 per cent of samples will lie within about 3 per cent of the population distribution on one side or the other. Translating this into real-life terms, let us suppose that the population is split exactly fifty–fifty between Labour and Conservative. Then 95 per cent of the random samples we draw from the population will show a distribution no further apart than forty-seven of one party to fifty-three of the other. The same point can be made if we start with the sample and try to make a guess about the population. If we find that the members of a sample we have taken divide exactly fifty–fifty into Labour and Conservative, then there is a 95 per cent chance (the odds, that is to say, are nineteen to one in our favour) that the electorate as a whole is somewhere between 47 per cent Labour to 53 per cent Conservative and 53 per cent Labour to 47 per cent Conservative. We cannot eliminate the margin of error entirely; but with sufficiently accurate sampling we can get it down to a matter of two or three per cent either way. This margin is known as "sampling error", and it is highly relevant to the second main criticism which is made of opinion polls.

2.   "Since the polls have managed to get the general election result wrong, why should I believe what they say at any other time?"

In 1948 the American opinion polls tipped the Republican candidate Thomas Dewey to win the presidential election, which was actually won by Democrat Harry Truman. In 1970 the British opinion polls forecast a Labour win and in February 1974 a Conservative victory. They were wrong both times, and their credibility was badly dented. After the 1970 election the pollsters spent a long time licking their wounds, and devised some modifications to their calculations to take account of the fact that they had all overestimated the Labour vote. Applying these modifications in February 1974, they promptly overestimated the Conservative vote instead.

In fact, the polls' record in general election predictions is much better than it looks. They appeared to do badly only because people, especially newspaper sub-editors, expected them to be able to do things which they could not possibly do. As we have said, the impossibility of avoiding sampling error means that a percentage figure given in an opinion poll can never guarantee to be closer than 2 or 3 per cent away from the true figure. But the margin between the two leading parties in British elections is almost always slender, and often within the 4 to 6 per cent range of sampling error. If a poll shows Labour as being 3 per cent ahead of the Conservatives, the true position could be anywhere between a dead heat and a 6 per cent Labour lead. In February 1974, as a matter of fact, the polls were almost spot on; they predicted a Conservative lead over Labour of 3 per cent, and there actually was one of 1 per cent. Labour won more *seats*, because of the way the votes were distributed, but the Conservatives won more votes – very close to the share the polls had predicted.

Opinion polls, therefore, are not too reliable as tipsters for general elections, because the result is usually so close that it falls within the range of sampling error. But this is not true of inter-election periods, when there is often a yawning chasm between the parties. The general trends in party support that are chronicled by the polls in between elections are undoubtedly fairly reliable. Like by-elections and local elections, they show a consistent pattern of the government of the day doing very badly in mid-term, and rallying as the next election approaches.

Politicians and the economy
Why, then, do all governments lose by-elections? "A government is

not supported a hundredth part so much by the constant, uniform, quiet prosperity of the country as by those damned spurs which Pitt used to have just in the nick of time." That comment was made by one disgruntled Whig to another about Tory successes in the 1790s, and it remains the most popular explanation for the pattern – which has certainly been recurring at least since 1886 – of by-election troughs followed by rallies preceding general elections. Governments manipulate politics, so it is argued, in order to make sure that they can take popular actions just before an election. In this they are helped by the fact that election dates are not fixed, as they are in the USA for example. So long as they do not go beyond the maximum permitted life of a parliament, prime ministers can choose the time of a general election to suit their party. A rational prime minister would always get unpopular measures through in the first two years of his administration, during which his party would slump in the opinion polls and lose badly in by-elections, and hope for an election-winning issue to tide him through the next election.

Election-winning issues can be very diverse. The Conservatives won the general election of 1900 on a tide of patriotic fervour for the Boer War. Harold Wilson's unexpected defeat in 1970 has been ascribed to disappointment at England's elimination from the World Cup in the quarter-final. Perhaps it is just as well that neither 1974 election took place in the summer. Scotland's Argentine disaster of 1978, on the other hand, may have hastened the downfall of the SNP. But the economy has always been seen as the main way of influencing election results. Before the last war it was rather like the weather – it might be bad or good, but politicians did not think they could do anything about it, or about its effects on their election chances. But in the last thirty years economic theory has changed. Governments accept it as part of their job to maintain full employment, and they believe that it is possible to manage the economy in various ways: increasing or decreasing the money supply, imposing or relaxing controls on spending, and so on. Both in 1955 and in 1959 the Conservatives produced a generous expansionist Budget just before they won the election and an austere restrictive one shortly after. Some pessimistic pro-Labour observers thought that the Conservatives had found the secret of staying in power for ever, by choosing an election date just after they had given the economy a "damned spurt in the nick of time". However, the trick just failed to work in 1964. After a trough of deep unpopularity in 1962 and 1963, the Conservatives again rallied in 1964, in which year there was yet another giveaway Budget. But they lost the 1964 general election to Labour by an overall majority of four.

It has since become clear, alas, that we live in too uncertain a world for governments to be able neatly to manipulate the economy and, through the economy, the election result. The economic booms and slumps of the 1960s and 1970s were much bigger than those of the 1950s. Both inflation and unemployment rose to higher levels than had been seen since the war. The cycle of by-elections, local elections and opinion polls also showed much more volatility than before. Perhaps the main reason was a growing divergence between what politicians promised the voters they could do (which related closely to what electors expected them to be able to do) and what they actually could do. This divergence has now become so acute that the whole of British politics is in great confusion.

Up to the last war politicians did not think they could do much to influence the economy. Nor, by and large, did voters expect them to. During the war many voters felt that the parties *ought* to try to secure full employment. Politicians shared this feeling, which was bolstered by the discovery that in the 1940s and 1950s they could. But it is very hard, some would say impossible, to deliver all the economic goods at the same time. Full employment is good; so is low inflation; so is a stable rate of exchange for the currency. As politicians are competing for votes, they must compete in their claims that they can achieve all these things. When the economy is growing, the difficulty of achieving all of them is concealed. But when, as after the quadrupling of world oil prices in 1973, the economy is bound to be stagnant, the gap between politicians' promises (which are also the electors' expectations) and politicians' performance becomes uncomfortably wide. This could be the main reason why the electoral cycle ended so differently in 1974. Instead of rallying to the government of the day, voters deserted both main parties in unprecedented numbers, not because they particularly liked the policies of the Liberals and Nationalists, but because neither main party could manage the economy in the comfortable way which helped the Conservatives to office in 1955, 1959, and very nearly in 1964.

This disillusionment also explains why the electoral troughs have got deeper. By-elections and local elections have been aptly labelled as "low salience" elections. Turnout is almost always lower than at general elections, and one of the biggest movements of votes at such elections is clearly abstention on the part of government supporters. This abstention was largely responsible for the huge swing to the Conservatives in polls and by-elections between 1966 and 1969. But here again we must not be confused by the word "swing". Labour voters did not "swing" to the Conservatives; they retreated to abstention. Nor did they move on from abstention (or minor party support) to the other side; by and large they returned to Labour in 1970.

It is still not clear how severely the dominance of the two major parties has been threatened. The minor-party surge that began in 1967 and reached full flood in 1974 retreated again in 1979, and Ulster is the only part of the UK which will indisputably never be the same again. But we have probably not seen the last of the Liberals and Scottish Nationalists. The gap between what politicians actually can do and what voters expect them to be able to do will remain wide, and third and fourth parties promising to do better will thus resurge from time to time. The 1979 general election, although in a sense it restored two-party dominance, left the question open; it was a dominance in seats rather than in votes, and the traditional social base of both parties was eroded and partly overlaid by regional factors (in all classes, the Conservatives did best in prosperous parts of the country and Labour did best in the north of England and Scotland). It also suggested a strange echo of the nineteenth century politics discussed in chapter 4: increasingly the Labour Party is the party of the big cities and the Conservatives the party of smaller towns and suburbs as well as the countryside. It is very appropriate that Mrs Thatcher should have come of shopkeeping forebears in Grantham. We may be witnessing not the rise of a new alignment but the awakening of a very old one.

6 The Voice of the People?

The meaning of the results

In the previous chapters we have studied the *process* of elections in some depth. Let us now look at the *outcome* of elections, the meaning of their results in the light of what we know about voting behaviour.

An important point is the relationship between political issues and election results. Both before and after a general election politicians often believe that there is a close link between the two, and this link is often expressed in terms of a "mandate". If a government's policy is being obstructed by the opposition or by external forces, it may go to the country in the hope of getting a mandate to carry on with its policy. After an election, governments often claim that their victory is evidence that they have a mandate for what they want to do. There are many examples of these claims at work in British political history. In 1910, for instance, the Liberal government was being constantly harassed by the Conservative-dominated House of Lords, who had thrown out the Budget of 1909. The government therefore went to the country to get the electorate's approval for its policies. It won both elections in 1910 (January and December) and thereafter claimed that it had a mandate for reforming the House of Lords. But this argument was turned on its head in a sophisticated (though unconvincing) way by some Tory peers, who argued that the House of Lords must continue to have the power to block ill-considered legislation, so that governments would be forced to go to the country and seek a mandate. Thus the House of Lords was the guarantor of popular control over tyrannical governments. (It was not explained, unfortunately, why the Lords never blocked Conservative tryanny, but only Liberal tyranny.)

Many years later, in early 1974, the Conservative government found itself, like its Liberal predecessor of 1909–10, forced into

79

having an election. With the miners banning overtime and about to strike against the Government's incomes policy, its only recourse was to call a general election in the hope of getting a mandate for its policy. In 1974, however, unlike 1910, the attempt failed. But both stories have one thing in common. They show that a government may launch an election on one issue, but it cannot keep it on course on that issue alone. In every election, even crisis elections like January 1910 and February 1974, other matters arise to obscure and overlay the original cause of the election. In 1910 electors were soon drawn away from the constitutional question to the standard issues of the day such as free trade versus protection and the government's record on dealing with unemployment. In 1974 the Conservatives calculated wrongly that they would sweep the country on the issue of "the Government versus the miners". It was true that public opinion was with them and against the miners. But, paradoxically, a majority of voters thought that Labour was better at "handling the unions"; and in any case, by the time polling day came round, they were much more worried about inflation and rising prices, and they thought that Labour was the best party to deal with these problems.

It seems, then, that governments which call elections in order to seek the electorate's support on one specific issue are doomed to disappointment. As one cynical commentator said, surveying the inconclusive results of the February 1974 election, "They (the Conservatives) asked a bloody silly question and they got a bloody silly answer". What about the other side of the question: the claim that governments have a mandate for the policies they put into effect once they have won an election? The claim seems reasonable enough, but it is open to two powerful objections.

The first is that governments hardly ever win over half the votes cast in a general election. Still less does any party ever secure the votes of half the *electorate*, bearing in mind that only about three-quarters of the electorate actually vote. The general elections of 1900, 1931 and 1935 are the only three this century in which the winning party (in each case the Conservatives) has taken over half the votes cast. Ironically, the largest share of the *electorate's* vote, taking abstainers into the calculation, to have been obtained by either major party since the war was the 40·3 per cent secured by the Labour Party in 1951. Since Labour got more votes, but fewer seats than the Conservatives in 1951, it lost that election. The lowest share of the electorate's votes to go to either major party since the war was the 26·1 per cent recorded by the Conservatives in October 1974; but the second lowest was the 28·6 per cent achieved by the Labour Party in the same election, though it narrowly obtained an overall majority in seats. Here is paradox indeed: the largest share of the electorate went to the Labour Party when it *lost* the 1951 election; the second smallest went to the same party when it *won* the October 1974 election. If talk of mandates is to bear any relationship to voting behaviour, the Labour opposition of 1951 to 1955 had a very much clearer mandate to introduce its policies than the Labour government of October 1974!

There is an even more fundamental problem with the notion of the mandate. One may say that the results of 1951 and 1974 were freaks, and that such paradoxes would not recur with normal elections (although it is unclear whether there will ever again be a "normal' election in this sense). But even after a "normal" election it is not at all safe to infer that, because voters have supported a party, they support its stand on the issues of its manifesto. Chapter 3 contains a great deal of evidence to show that this is not the case. Many electors actually prefer the policies put forward by the opposite party to those of the one they vote for. Yet, as we have said, this is not necessarily irrational. Voters may neither know nor care what the parties intend to do with NATO or Africa; it is a matter of in-difference for such voters if their own views are opposed to their party's views. But some things – prices, social services, immigration, for instance – concern voters very vitally indeed, and they are much less likely to support a party which does not share their views on these questions. Only for issues in this category, issues which, in the jargon of political science, are "salient" for most voters, does it make sense to say that governments have mandates for their policies. In fact, political issues can be divided into three categories, in ascending order of the electorate's awareness of them.

1 Issues where voters have no real opinion at all. Some of the examples we gave in chapter 3 come into this category. Many questions are of the very greatest importance to political activists. Should the money supply be restricted as a means of curbing in-flation? On what basis should government grants to local authorities be calculated? These, and hundreds like them, are politically controversial questions, but they are also highly technical. Politicians, administrators and pressure groups have opinions on them, but ordinary voters can scarcely be expected to.

2   Issues where voters have non-salient opinions. This is an interesting intermediate category. The state of public opinion about national-isation of industry provides an example. Over the years from 1950 to the present day, survey after survey has shown that the great majority of voters are consistently opposed to extensions of public ownership. Sometimes even a majority of Labour voters are found to be opposed to it. It would therefore be perverse for any Labour politician to claim that he had a popular mandate for further nationalisation (which is not to say that the claim is not made). Nevertheless, such a person could fairly point out that virtually everybody *knows* that the Labour Party favours further national-isation, but that this does not deter many voters from supporting Labour, even if they are personally against more public ownership. Nationalisation is an issue of low salience; electors know what they (and the parties) think, but they do not greatly care. A Labour government has no "mandate" for nationalisation; but neither has a Conservative one against it.

3   Issues where voters have salient opinions. Butler and Stokes, who have conducted the most careful research on these subjects, found only three issues which the voters as a whole thought important and on which they had firm views. These were: social services, industrial relations and coloured immigration. A substantial majority of voters want higher spending on social services, especially pensions and housing; most people think strikes are a "very serious" problem, and those who are generally against them outnumber by four to one those who are generally for them; and a steady 80 to 85 per cent of the electorate thinks that "too many immigrants have been let into this country". On all these issues opinion is skewed – that is, there are far more people on one side than on the other. A party which could consistently pick the winning side on all these issues would have a strong chance of winning every election. But, in fact, the match between these salient issues and party manifestoes is curious and rather weak.

Improving the social services is like being for good and against evil. Most people are on the same side. Faced with all parties promising to improve the social services, the electorate has fairly consistently believed that the Labour Party is most likely to put its promises into practice. This has been of considerable help to Labour at election times. On industrial relations the position is more confused. More voters believe that Labour has a "better approach to strikes" than the Conservatives, although more still think there is no difference between the parties. In 1969, when Harold Wilson and Barbara Castle launched their ill-fated proposals, ironically titled *In Place of Strife*, which were intended to reform the structure of trade unions, they knew they had public opinion behind them. But the picture of public opinion was very opaque by the time it filtered through to the Parliamentary Labour Party, many of whose members were as unhappy as the trade unions themselves at the proposals. As neither the unions nor the PLP would stand for it, *In Place of Strife* was abandoned in June 1969. Ironically, it would have been one of the few issues on which Wilson could meaningfully have claimed a popular mandate for his policy.

The position regarding restriction of entry to coloured Commonwealth immigrants is different again. Both parties have been reluctant to side with public opinion; both have been much less keen to restrict immigration than the voters who support them. At first, this was perhaps largely the result of ignorance. The parties were unaware how deep the electorate's hostility to coloured immigration actually was. Later, it arose more from the feeling that it was right to have a humane policy towards immigrants and their dependants, whatever the electorate thought, in defiance of public opinion if necessary.

This illustrates a more general point about the relationship between election results, party programmes, and public opinion. We have seen that parties do not win elections because of what is in their manifestoes, that therefore it rarely makes sense for them to claim a mandate for their policies except in the most general way, and that the relationship between party programmes and public opinion is tenuous, to say the least of it. There are two main reasons why the links between parties and public opinion are not closer. One is that the structure of parties actually insulates politicians from understanding what the state of public opinion really is. Politicians spend much of their time talking to other politicians or party activists, or reading the opinions of political journalists in a handful of "quality" papers. But the views of these people, even if they are grass-roots constituency activists, are often wildly unrepresentative of the views of the electorate as a whole. For instance, Mr Bernard Levin, the *Times* columnist, campaigned actively and vociferously in the early 1970s for a political realignment, with sensible men of the centre (such as himself) forming a new party against the extremist dominated Labour and Conservative Parties. This was all very well; but columns in *The Times*, however witty, do not create political parties. Mr Levin was somewhat imprisoned in myths of his own creation in believing that his writings were having a massive effect on public opinion; but that was not so absurd as the belief, seriously canvassed in the Sunday papers, that the "Bernard Levin block vote" was swinging to the Liberals and endangering (especially) the Labour Party. In fact, of course, *The Times* only reaches a tiny minority of the electorate, and the views of its readers and writers are in no way typical of public opinion.

Theories of representation and the referendum

Sometimes, then, politicians simply do not know what public opinion is; but sometimes they deliberately choose to ignore it. This is true of immigration control, and it is also true of capital punishment, which public opinion favours but politicians oppose. (The House of Commons voted to abolish capital punishment for murder in 1957 and all attempts to reintroduce it so far have failed.) Usually they justify their position by reference to the views of Edmund Burke, the eighteenth-century conservative writer. Burke thought that a representative ought not to act as a "delegate", that is, as the mouthpiece for his electors in pressing for whatever they demanded; he ought to exercise his own judgment and make his own mind up on the issues of the day. Burke's view of representation appeals most to Conservatives, but it is not unknown for Labour MPs to express it as well.

A clear example was a speech by Brian Walden, Labour MP for Birmingham Ladywood at the time. In December 1974 just after twenty people had been murdered in his own constituency by terrorist bombs thrown into two pubs, Walden introduced a resolution opposing the restoration of capital punishment for terrorist offences. He conceded the point that public opinion was in favour of restoration. "Any expression of public opinion must be a matter of grave concern to this House. It must form part of our judgment – part of our judgment, but not the whole. Are we a House of delegates?"

Walden, like Burke, answered this question in the negative. The House of Commons, he went on, was "a body ultimately responsible to the people but mandated by no one. . . . I shall never change that opinion. I shall ever hold to it. When it dies, parliamentary democracy will die with it and one may make one's peace with plebiscitary democracy, that friend of tyrants and demagogues. (Hon. Members: 'Hear, Hear'.)"

This is an extreme statement, made on an emotional occasion, but it expresses views that in practice virtually every MP endorses. Many would argue fervently that they favour greater popular participation in government, and this was one of the leading arguments put forward in favour of the 1975 referendum on Common Market membership. But hardly any are consistent populists – that is, people who will support public opinion whatever it may be. When public opinion is on their side, MPs are naturally proud to point to it in support of them; when it is not, they must either turn a blind eye to it, or adopt Burke's dictum that they are not delegates, but representatives. Elections are important in Burke's theory and its modern developments. When Walden mentioned, in the speech just quoted, that MPs are ultimately responsible to the people, he was putting forward the conventional view that, if an MP's constituents do not like his views they can always dismiss him at the next election, and adding by implication that they should not expect any further role in government. A more novel view is. implied, however, by the Common Market referendum of June 1975, and the Scottish and Welsh devolution referenda of March 1979.

They were not the first referenda to be held in Britain. In Scotland and Wales, for instance, there have been quite a number of polls on licensing issues. Scottish electors could vote for their area to have public houses, or a restricted number of licences, or to go "dry" entirely. In parts of Wales, there are still polls every seven years on whether public houses should open on Sundays. At the time of writing, parts of Caernarvon, Anglesey, Merioneth and Cardigan still keep alive nineteenth-century politics by shutting the pubs on Sundays. A more substantial precedent was the Northern Ireland Border poll of 1973, when voters were asked whether they wished Northern Ireland to remain part of the United Kingdom, or to become part of the Republic of Ireland. The result was foreordained: a massive majority for remaining part of the UK. The Protestant majority was wholly in favour; the Catholic minority, which might well have been split, in fact heeded the advice of its political leaders to boycott the poll since, whatever they did, there could be only one possible result.

On a much larger scale was the first ever full-scale national referendum to be held in Britain: the poll conducted in June 1975 to decide whether Britain should remain a member of the European Economic Community. It was the culmination of a very long saga. Britain's first application to join was made by the Conservative government in 1961 and was turned down by President de Gaulle's veto. The Labour Party, under Hugh Gaitskell, was then anti-Market. In 1967, however, the Wilson government made another application to join, which was again unsuccessful. The third attempt did succeed. It was made by the Heath government which came to power in 1970, and Britain became part of the EEC as from 1 January 1973.

The Labour Party was naturally suspicious of a deal negotiated by its opponents, and called for a renegotiation of the terms of entry. This formula half-concealed a serious division between pro- and anti-Marketeers within the party. To conciliate the antis, who held a dominant position in the Labour Party conference, the Labour leaders promised that the renegotiated terms would be submitted to the electorate to enable them to make the final decision about remaining in the Common Market. When Labour returned to power in 1974 the renegotiation began, and it was concluded at a "summit" meeting of all the EEC leaders in Dublin in March 1975.

The referendum had a strange effect on British party politics. The Labour Party was bitterly and deeply divided, the majority of the party outside Parliament being anti-Market while the majority of the Cabinet was pro. But every other party was divided also. The Conservatives had an anti-Market minority; so did the Liberals, and even the SNP, whose public position was one of strident opposition to the EEC and all its works, were privately optimistic about the prospects of money from EEC funds for Scottish development. Thus no party could unitedly campaign on either side. Voters who were used to taking their cues from their party on political issues got no guidance. Propaganda was channelled through two umbrella organisations, one pro and one anti, who each distributed a leaflet (at government expense) to every household in the country. These leaflets were accompanied by a government statement in favour of accepting the renegotiated terms.

Throughout the campaign a "Yes" majority seemed the more likely. The opinion polls implied that the margin in favour would be substantial, but they were widely disbelieved because of their alleged failure to predict the February 1974 election result correctly. The *Guardian* carried the eve-of-poll headline, *Polls predict two-to-one Yes vote – and hold their breath*. The polls were quite right (not that they got any credit for being right). The actual vote was in favour of staying in by 67 per cent to 33 per cent, and the overall turnout was 64 per cent. There were some regional variations: Scotland, and some strongly Labour areas in England and Wales, had below-average "Yes" majorities, reflecting the "No" advice coming from most leaders of the SNP and the Labour Party. But no area except Shetland and the Western Isles actually produced an anti-Market majority.

Within four years, another two important referenda took place. The Labour government of 1974 had promised to introduce devolution of some government functions to assemblies in Scotland and Wales. But they faced an "English backlash" on their own backbenches which culminated in the defeat of the Scotland and Wales Bill in 1976. To mollify the anti-devolutionists the government promised that referenda would be held in Scotland and Wales before devolution was implemented. This helped the government to get separate Scotland and Wales Acts passed in 1978, but not without further mauling: rebel backbenchers inserted a clause requiring the government to lay a repeal order before the House of Commons if fewer than 40 per cent of the registered electorate in Scotland and/or Wales voted "Yes".

The referenda were held on 1 March 1979. The Welsh electors, in the words of the *Guardian*, "booted the Welsh Assembly into Cardigan Bay": the vote was 80/20 against an assembly and only 11·8 per cent out of the Welsh electorate voted "Yes". The Scottish result was narrowly favourable (51·6 to 48·4 per cent of the vote) but came nowhere near the "40 per cent barrier": only 32·5 per cent of the electorate voted "Yes". The constitutional ramifications might have been intriguing, but debate was cut short by the Conservative victory at the 1979 general election, which was accompanied by a promise to repeal the Scotland Act.

These events reopened some old arguments for and against referenda in general. In principle, every democrat must agree that it is a good thing that the people should be consulted. Where the issue is clearcut, and everybody can be expected to have an opinion, the referendum is an excellent device for ensuring more democratic government. This is true in the case of the licensing polls, and it was true in the case of the Northern Ireland Border poll. (The outcome of that was certainly democratic in the sense that it showed what the majority wanted; whether the majority is tolerant, or fair to the minority, is another matter entirely.) To a degree, it was also true of the Common Market. Of the countries considering joining the EEC in 1972, Norway, Denmark and Ireland all had referenda on the subject. In Denmark the vote was for joining, and in Ireland, where the referendum came after the government's decision, it confirmed that decision to enter. In Norway, however, the vote was to stay out, and Norway, accordingly, did not join. The British referendum, therefore, was in one of its aspects an effort to give the British people the same say on the Common Market as their counterparts in Norway, Denmark and Ireland.

In practice, of course, reasons of political expediency also loomed large. The impending split in the Labour Party over the Common Market had been obvious for several years before 1974. The referendum was obviously a useful device for minimising the effect of the split. But it left the government open to two main criticisms. First, was it not abdicating the duty of government, namely to govern? Secondly, if experts could not agree on the highly technical questions of whether we stood to gain or lose from continued membership, how could the public be expected to know the right answer?

The first criticism was aptly made by a Conservative MP during the debate about capital punishment and terrorism. Referring to Walden's speech, quoted on pp. 84–85, Mrs Jill Knight said: "If I understand the hon. member for Ladywood (Walden) correctly, he has told his Front Bench that there is no point in having a referendum because we should not work like that and we should not govern in that way. I hope that the government will listen, but I doubt it." This was a party political debating point, but none the less effective for that, because it exposed an inconsistency in the government's position. If you have a referendum on the Common Market, why not one on restoring capital punishment? The obvious, and unacceptable, answer is: because a referendum on capital punishment will go the wrong way – that is, it will produce a large majority in favour, whereas almost all Labour MPs and at least a large minority of Conservatives are against it. Anybody who holds this view is surely a manipulator, not a democrat. Whatever else it may be, it cannot be democratic to be in favour of referenda where the results will go your way, or paper over the cracks in the unity of your party, but to be against them where the result will go against you. The only arguments worth listening to are consistent ones. Either one must be consistently in favour of the referendum, whatever the consequences, or consistently against it.

To be consistently in favour of referenda is a quite acceptable position to adopt. It is the position of consistent populism: "I am in favour of whatever a majority of the voters want." One problem is what to do when two or more different majorities want incompatible things. Every majority, after all, consists of different people. And even if it did not, people often want a range of things which are very difficult to provide simultaneously: full employment, low inflation and a stable currency, for instance. Referenda cannot establish *priorities* between different desirable things. We live in what economists call a world of scarce resources. There is not enough time, money or land for everybody to do all he wants. Therefore all political systems must decide what priorities come first and what must be sacrificed, must decide at the margin between building a new school, or a new hospital, or investing in industrial machinery, or simply withdrawing money from the economy to try to discourage inflation. It is difficult to see how these priorities could be resolved through the referendum.

However, most politicians are not consistent populists (though quite a few are inconsistent populists). There are some policies they will want to pursue even if public opinion is against them. Each politician will have his own list: it might include opposing capital punishment, say, or enforcing good race relations, or abandoning subsidies to nationalised industries. He will reserve the right to argue for policies he supports even if he knows the majority of the electorate disagree. This is the position taken by Walden in the speech from which we have quoted, and it is really inconsistent with the desire for referenda, except on issues to which politicians themselves are indifferent, or nearly so. All the arguments which can be used to justify a referendum on the EEC can also be used to justify one on capital punishment. If MPs were logical creatures they would have to favour both or neither.

The other common criticism of the referendum is less serious. It is that the issues are too obscure or confusing for voters to be able to make an intelligent assessment of them. This is obviously true of many political issues; we have seen that there are many important questions on which the majority of people have no opinion at all. Hence not every political controversy could be settled by referendum. But there is a range of issues on which most people do have a stable opinion. Many of them, admittedly, are not as straightforward as they look. On the Common Market, for instance, the technical argument on whether or not membership was economically beneficial very quickly became strictly a matter for experts only. But if (and it is a big if) fair arrangements are made for ensuring that voters hear both sides of the question, it seems reasonable to expect them to be able to make up their minds on matters of principle.

The Scottish and Welsh referenda raised further questions. First, who is to count as the relevant part of the electorate? The English are surely entitled to views of how the UK should be governed just as much as the Scots and Welsh. But there was no referendum in England on the Scotland and Wales Acts. But suppose there had been; and that a majority of the English voted against Scottish devolution while a majority of Scots voted for it? That would have been a contradiction which no democratic theory can resolve. Second, could the 40 per cent rule be justified? Its supporters pointed out that in the event 32·5 per cent of the Scottish electorate voted "Yes", 30·4 per cent voted "No", but that abstainers, at 37·1 per cent, outnumbered both – hardly the basis for fundamental constitutional change. On the other hand, Westminster politicians have never been keen to apply anything like a 40 per cent rule to themselves. Not a single government elected since 1945 has ever received 40 per cent of the electorate's votes. Only one party has ever broken that barrier in a postwar general election. In 1951, as noted earlier, the Labour Party got the support of 40·3 per cent of the electorate – but *lost* the election, because the Conservatives won more seats.

Representative or populist democracy?

For the foreseeable future, no doubt, elections will continue to play a much bigger role than referenda in the government of Britain. But the points which have just been raised – what one might call the dispute between populist democracy and representative democracy – are part of a very ancient controversy. The most trenchant critic of the sort of representative democracy which exists in Britain today was the great French philosopher Jean-Jacques Rousseau. Although he wrote two hundred years ago, nobody since has more pithily expressed the populist criticism of representative democracy.

> The deputies of the people [i.e. MPs] thus are not and cannot be its representatives. They are merely its agents. They cannot make any binding agreements. Any law which the people have not ratified in person is invalid: it is not a law at all. The people of England think they are free. They are gravely mistaken. They are free only when they are electing members of parliament. As soon as the members have been elected, the people are enslaved – they are nothing.[1]

In Rousseau's view, the people are free only when they are governing themselves. They cannot be represented. The only acceptable role for MPs is to act as agents of the people – to do what the people have instructed them, and to submit any proposed law for popular ratification. If MPs act independently of their electors, then the people are not governing themselves, and are not, in Rousseau's sense, "free". Rousseau's views, which are thus the direct opposite of Burke's, are shared by many modern radicals. How can Britain be called a democracy when, at most, our participation in politics amounts to voting perhaps fifteen times in our lifetimes at a general election? How can it be called a democracy when voters have no control over the MPs they elect?

These are very compelling arguments, and, since they challenge the whole basis of the system we live under, a large number of critics have tried to rebut them. A common criticism is that populist democracy as envisaged by Rousseau could not work in any community larger than about 10,000 people. The only Rousseau-style democracies which have ever worked were in Ancient Greece, especially Athens. Here the assembly of all the citizens genuinely took decisions, which were carried out by a council whose members were chosen by lot from among the citizens. Two things were

---

[1] J. J. Rousseau, *Du Contrat Social*, Book III ch. 15 (Author's translation).

needed to make this system work: a small city and a large number of slaves. The biggest possible public meeting at which it makes sense to say that those present take decisions, rather than merely listen to speakers, is perhaps 2,000 strong. And a public meeting which genuinely takes decisions is bound to spend a very long time taking them. Direct democracy depends on the citizens being interested and willing to spend a great deal of time participating in politics. This is only conceivable if the citizens have a great deal of spare time, which in turn could only happen if they were free of day-to-day chores. Ancient Greek democracy depended on having slaves to do the washing up. In ancient Athens citizens were several times out-numbered by resident aliens and by slaves, who of course had no voting rights.

Rousseau's defenders may retort that this is not much of an argument. Modern technology has given all classes of citizens an amount of spare time that would have been inconceivable in the past. Direct democracy can work, they might add, as shown by the growth of communes in modern Western societies, where groups of people live together and take all the decisions that affect them by genuinely democratic means, without devices like elections and representation. Rousseau-style democracy, commune-style self-government, is the only true form of free government, and it can be extended to political affairs through "community politics" where decisions about the street are taken by those living in the street.

Unfortunately this argument does not reckon with the complexity of modern society. As Ralf Dahrendorf, former EEC Commissioner, has put it: "Community politics cannot guarantee a sensible policy for the siting of nuclear power stations." A series of streets next to one another could each operate as a self-governing commune; but how do they get together to decide (say) a housing policy for the whole city, to say nothing of a nuclear power policy for the whole nation? They would have to appoint delegates to the joint meeting of all the communes that took decisions about housing or nuclear power. But representative government would then have come in again through the back door. Effectively, decisions on policies and priorities would once again be taken by elected representatives. For, however strictly the delegates were instructed to report back to the commune that sent them before taking decisions, they would inevitably be involved in bargaining and compromises that would be too complex to be reported back if any decisions were ever to be taken. However we look at the problem it does not seem as if we can escape the fact that democracy, in a modern industrial society, must be representative democracy.

But the question of the relationship between elections, electors and elected remains highly controversial. According to an influential school of conservative writers, not only does democracy in the real world in no way resemble Rousseau's ideal but it is highly undesirable that it should even try to develop in that direction. This new theory is worth understanding and disentangling, for it lies at the heart of the modern argument about democracy and the role of the electorate.

The most important writer was the Austrian economist Joseph Schumpeter, who wrote, in an influential book published in 1942: "The democratic method is that institutional arrangement for arriving at political decisions in which individuals acquire the power to decide by means of a competitive struggle for the people's vote."[1] In other words, democracy is not government by the people. It is government by one set of politicians who derive their right to do so from the fact that in a free election they have got more votes than any other set of politicians. Put as bluntly as this, Schumpeter's definition has always been highly controversial because he seems to deny many of the cherished ideals of democracy. Furthermore, not only does he insist that democracy *is* no more than competition among politicians for the right to rule, but he also asserts that it *ought* not to be extended to embrace the sort of popular rule envisaged by Rousseau and his modern followers. One may agree with the *is* but still wish to quarrel with the *ought*, and the two parts of the argument must be treated separately.

The definition of democracy as a system where politicians acquire the right to rule by winning elections has many merits. It pinpoints the difference between countries which most people call democracies – such as Britain, the USA and India – from those which most people do not – Brazil and Guinea, for instance. The first group have free elections in which anybody may stand; the second do not. Friends of every sort of undemocratic regime naturally play down the importance of free elections, but there is no getting away from it. It may well be true that (say) Sekou Touré of Guinea or the leaders of the Communist Party of the Soviet Union rule

[1] J. A. Schumpeter, *Capitalism, Socialism and Democracy*, Allen & Unwin, 1954 edn, p. 269.

their respective countries with the support of public opinion, but we have no way of knowing. Even if such regimes are popular with their citizens, that is not to say that they are democracies. Many things done by the Emperor Nero, including the persecution of Christians, had the warm support of the Roman people, but that did not make his regime a democracy.

Schumpeter's definition may seem to be silent on an essential feature of democracy, namely the need for politicians to do what the electorate wants them to do. This is partially covered, however, by the notion of competition. A party will not win an election unless voters both agree with its policies (or some of them at least) and believe that it will try to put them into force if elected. And once elected, a government must not forget that it needs to try to win the next election as well. Whatever it may do in the short run, it must face a reckoning within five years when the next election comes round.

It might be felt that this is inadequate: that it would be more democratic if politicians were required to take more notice of public opinion in between elections – through the referendum for example. The point is a good one, so long as it is recognised that one must be either a consistent supporter of referenda or not a supporter at all. It is either simple-minded or hypocritical to favour a referendum on the Common Market but not one on capital punishment. If politicians are entirely free to decide when to have a referendum and when not to, this does not make a regime more democratic than if it had no provision for referenda. But if there is a power of "initiative" – that is, if a certain proportion of the electorate has the automatic right to demand a referendum on a subject of their choice – then we may justly say that a regime is more democratic than if there is no such right.

But the really controversial part of Schumpeter's argument is that which says that democracies *ought* not to become more participatory: that it is undesirable that voters should take any part in politics beyond voting in general elections every so often. Here the conservatives are making two points, one very good and one rather weak. The weaker point lies in the claim that voters are not sufficiently intelligent or sophisticated to understand political issues deeply enough to participate more actively than they do. But, as we argued in chapter 3, the fears which some writers have expressed about the stupidity or irrationality of the electorate are probably much exaggerated. Schumpeter is on much firmer ground when he points out that a democracy is not necessarily liberal, tolerant or fair to minorities. He speaks of a hypothetical democracy which persecuted Christians and Jews and burnt witches. Surely, he argues, we would not approve of these practices just because they were democratically agreed? This is a most important point. It is quite possible to have free and fair elections which lead to an undesirable outcome. This was almost the position in Northern Ireland for fifty years. A section of the population, the Catholics, did not enjoy full civil rights or fair job opportunities; they belonged to a state which many of them did not wish to exist at all. But this situation was reached quite democratically as a result of elections in which the majority of voters supported politicians who freely continued their policies of systematic discrimination against the Catholic community. (Admittedly, Northern Ireland elections were not always fair, as there was gerrymandering of constituency boundaries and substantial impersonation of dead and absent voters. But even completely fair elections would have had virtually the same result, because Protestants outnumber Catholics by two to one.) In the Deep South of the USA, similarly, for many years a white majority has systematically discriminated against a black minority. Democracy is not, of itself, any guarantor of minority rights.

All this is irrefutable, and it is surprising and disappointing that many people find it difficult to understand. A democracy governed by free elections is, admittedly, often the best way to ensure a free and tolerant society. Representatives of a majority are much less likely to behave in an arbitrary and intolerant way if they know that after some future election they may be in a minority; they do not want to risk having the tables turned on them. To that extent democracy is a valuable check against unfair discrimination. But the check does not exist if the nature and size of the majority and minority groups are constant and unlikely to change. Protestants will outnumber Catholics in Northern Ireland, and whites outnumber blacks in the Deep South, for the foreseeable future. So there is no check on their behaviour caused by any feeling that they might themselves become the persecuted minority in future. Democracy has many merits, but it cannot do everything. Free elections are a *necessary* condition for fair government, but far from a *sufficient* condition.

In this chapter we have ranged far and wide in discussing some of the implications of having a representative democracy governed by free elections, and some of the possible alternatives. This is only one aspect of a large and fascinating topic. If, when next a reader watches a general election on TV, or reads the latest opinion polls or is "knocked-up" by a local election canvasser, he stops to reflect on the complex business of elections in which all these activities play their part, then this book may have achieved some small purpose.

Appendix

Proportional representation with the single transferable vote.

A youth club which contains sixty boys and forty girls needs a committee of five. There are ten candidates: five boys and five girls. It is known that all the boys will prefer male candidates and all the girls female ones. It is hoped that the result of the election will reflect the sex balance in the club.

The first step is to find the quota: $\dfrac{\text{number of votes} \quad +1}{\text{number of seats} +1}$

$$Q = \frac{100 +1}{5 +1}$$

$= 17 \cdot 7$ (which can be rounded *down* to 17, as there is no chance of 6 candidates getting 17 first preference votes each)

Any child with 17 votes is elected.
The counts are as follows:

	Count							
Candidate	1st	2nd	3rd	4th	5th	6th	7th	8th
Jim	22 – E	E	E	E	E	E	E	E
John	14	14	14+1=15	15	15	15	15	
Tom	12+3=15		15+3=18 – E	E	E	E	E	
Dick	8	8	8+2=10+1=11		11	11+6=17 – E		
Harry	4+2= 6	6	eliminated					
Mary	8	8	8	8	8+1= 9	eliminated		
Ann	13	13+2=15	15	15	15+4=19 – E E			
Susan	6	6+1= 7	7	7	eliminated			
Kate	10	10	10	10	10+6=16+5=21 – E E			
Jane	3	3	eliminated					

Three boys are elected: Jim, Tom and Dick
Two girls are elected: Ann and Kate

97

The transfer of votes operate as follows. After the first count only Jim has been elected. His surplus of 5 goes 3 to Tom and 2 to Harry (2nd count). Nobody has reached the quota, so Jane is eliminated; 2 of her votes go to Ann and 1 to Susan (3rd count). Still nobody has reached the quota, so Harry is eliminated. 1 vote goes to John, 3 to Tom and 2 to Dick (4th count). Tom is now elected with a surplus of 1, which is redistributed to Dick (5th count). Again nobody has reached the quota, so Susan is eliminated; 1 of her votes goes to Mary and 6 to Kate (6th count). Nobody thus reaches the quota, so Mary is eliminated; 4 votes go to Ann and 5 to Kate (7th count). They are both elected, leaving between them a surplus of 6, all of which go to Dick (8th count). Dick is therefore elected as the fifth member.

Note especially what happens between the 7th and 8th counts. Two boys are still in the running – John and Dick. John has been leading all the way through the counting, yet in the last ballot Dick sweeps in because he gets all 6 surplus votes from the two successful girl candidates. Obviously, John likes football and boozing with the lads; whereas Dick is a ladies' man who appeals to the girls. In the last count, it was the candidates with more appeal to the opposite camp who won. This is how STV benefits "moderates" and harms "extremists" – if the terms can be used in this context. For John substitute "Loyalist" and for Dick substitute "Alliance" or "moderate Protestant" and you will see exactly how it was that STV benefited moderates in the Northern Ireland Assembly elections of 1973.

Further reading

The most important book about elections in Britain is the massive work by D. E. Butler and D. Stokes, *Political Change in Britain* (Macmillan, 2nd edition, 1974; Penguin edition also available). This is long and, in places, difficult to follow, but it is full of good things for the reader who perseveres. *Political Representation and Elections in Britain* by P. G. J. Pulzer (Allen and Unwin, 3rd edition, 1975) is shorter and easier but also contains a sophisticated discussion of elections and voting behaviour. Another short treatment is *Voters, Parties and Leaders* by J. Blondel (Penguin, 2nd edition, 1969).

The above books deal with most or all the topics covered in the present book. More specialised books, dealing with particular aspects of elections, may be listed under the chapter headings of this book.

Chapter 1. Elections: how and why

Alone or in collaboration, Dr David Butler has written a study of every British general election since 1950. They are indispensable for the reader who wants to know what an election campaign is like from day to day. The most recent in the series are D. E. Butler and D. Kavanagh, *The British*

General Election of February 1974 (Macmillan 1974), D. E. Butler and D. Kavanagh, *The British General Election of October 1974* (Macmillan 1975) and D. E. Butler and U. Kitzinger, *The 1975 Referendum* (Macmillan 1976). There will be another volume, also by David Butler and Denis Kavanagh, on the 1979 general election. A more compact study of the 1974 elections is H. R. Penniman (ed.), *Britain at the Polls: the parliamentary elections of 1974* (American Enterprise Institute, Washington DC, 1975).

By contrast, the American way of doing things can be studied in a series of volumes by Theodore H. White, *The Making of the President, 1964, 1968* and *1972* (Cape).

Chapter 2. The Electoral System

There is a handy summary of electoral systems in W. J. M. Mackenzie, *Free Elections* (Allen and Unwin, 1958), and a full treatment linked with a passionate advocacy of STV in E. Lakeman, *How Democracies Vote* (Faber, 1970).

For AMS see *Report of the Hansard Society Commission on Electoral Reform* (Hansard Society for Parliamentary Government, 1976).

Chapter 3. Are Voters Rational?

The pioneer survey of Greenwich is still worth reading: M. Benney, A. Gray and R. Pear, *How People Vote* (Routledge, 1956). There is a good brief discussion of the controversy in W. G. Runciman, *Social Science and Political Theory* (Cambridge University Press, 2nd edition, 1969), and a vigorous argument in Samuel Brittan's book *Left and Right, the Bogus Dilemma* (Secker and Warburg, 1968).

The puzzle "why vote at all?" was raised, but not settled, in a brilliant and challenging theoretical book: *An Economic Theory of Democracy* by Anthony Downs (Harper & Row, New York, 1957)

Chapter 4. Voting Behaviour

Most of the material in chapters 4 and 5 is drawn from the work of Butler and Stokes. But see also R. T. McKenzie and A. Silver, *Angels in Marble* (Heinemann, 1968) on working-class Conservatives, and J. Goldthorpe and others, *The Affluent Worker: political attitudes and behaviour* (Cambridge University Press, 1968).

Chapter 5. Swings and Roundabouts

A lot of the balderdash talked about the opinion polls (notably by politicians) is dispelled in *Political Opinion Polls* by F. Teer and J. Spence (Hutchinson, 1973).

Chapter 6. The Voice of the People?

A great deal has been written about the theory of representative democracy and its rivals in more than two centuries of argument about it. Two classic texts are J. S. Mill, *Considerations on Representative Government* (1861; several modern editions) and J-J. Rousseau *The Social Contract* (1762;

several translations). For a sample of the modern controversy, try J. A. Schumpeter's *Capitalism, Socialism, and Democracy* (Allen and Unwin, revised edition, 1954, chapters 21 to 23); R. A. Dahl, *A Preface to Democratic Theory* (University of Chicago Press, 1956) for an American viewpoint; and P. Bachrach, *The Theory of Democratic Elitism* (University of London Press, 1969) as the best of a not very good bunch of attacks on Schumpeter's pessimistic conservatism.

Other topics

Finally, some books on topics which keep cropping up:

Northern Ireland

There is no satisfactory book on Northern Ireland politics for the student. Almost everything is out of date, or heavily biased, or both. Still the best general book is Richard Rose's *Governing without Consensus* (Faber, 1971). Although written before the troubles broke out, it is astonishingly prophetic. Conor Cruise O'Brien's *States of Ireland* (latest edition, Panther Books, 1974) manages brilliantly to be passionate without being biased; it is the best book yet written about the Northern Ireland troubles, but it could be mystifying to a reader who does not already have some knowledge of Irish history and politics. It is neatly balanced by A. T. Q. Stewart, *The Narrow Ground* (Faber, 1977) which substitutes weak orange-tinted spectacles for O'Brien's weak green-tinted ones.

Party history and ideology

There are two useful books by Henry Pelling: *The Origins of the Labour Party* (Oxford University Press, new edition, 1965) and *A Short History of the Labour Party* (Macmillan, 6th edition, 1979).

For the Conservatives, read Robert Blake, *The Conservative Party from Peel to Churchill* (Eyre & Spottiswoode, 1970): the best, though not the most recent treatment. There is also *A Short History of the Liberal Party, 1900–76* by Chris Cook (Macmillan, 1976).

Ambitious readers may enjoy the challenge of studying an important, but demanding, book which attempts to describe and account for the development of modern party ideologies: S. H. Beer, *Modern British Politics* (Faber, 2nd edition, 1969).

Elections are happening all the time, and books on the subject quickly get out of date. Fortunately, the standard of discussion and reporting of elections in national newspapers and on television is now quite high. Opinion polls regularly appear in several papers, including the *Daily Telegraph*, *Daily Mail*, and the London *Evening Standard*. The most intelligent Press discussions of election results and voting behaviour are often in the *Sunday Times*; and the television presentation of general election results has now achieved a high degree of expertise.

Index